# The Philippine Leader and the American Soldier
## Perspectives on America's Journey into Imperialism

BY
Emilio Aguinaldo
AND
Needom N. Freeman

This edition contains the complete and unabridged manuscripts of *True Version of the Philippine Revolutio*n, by Don Emilio Aguinaldo y Famy (published in 1899) and *A Soldier in the Philippines*, by Needom N. Freeman (published in 1901). All content not in the public domain is original to this edition. Content in the public domain includes the manuscript and the cover image.

Copyright © 2020 by C. Wade Naney

All rights reserved. No part of the original content or design of this book may be reproduced in any form or by any means, electronic or mechanical. Printed in the United States of America.

ISBN: 9798554024504

grindlpress.com

## CONTENTS

TRUE VERSION OF THE PHILIPPINE REVOLUTION ................................ 7
    I. The Revolution of 1896 ................................................. 11
    II. The Treaty of Peace of Biak-na-bató ........................... 13
    III. Negotiations ................................................................. 15
    IV. The Revolution of 1898 ............................................... 24
    V. The Dictatorial Government ....................................... 26
    VI. The First Triumphs ...................................................... 28
    VII. The Philippine Flag ..................................................... 30
    VIII. Expedition to Bisayas ................................................. 31
    IX. The Steamer "Compania de Filipinas" ....................... 31
    X. The Proclamation of Independence ........................... 32
    XI. The Spanish Commission ........................................... 34
    XII. More American Troops ............................................... 38
    XIII. The 13th August .......................................................... 39
    XIV. First Clouds ................................................................. 40
    XV. Vain Hopes .................................................................. 42
    XVI. The American Commission ....................................... 44
    XVII. Impolitic acts .............................................................. 45
    XVIII. The Mixed Commission ............................................. 48
    XIX. Outbreak of Hostilities ............................................... 49

IMAGES OF THE WAR ................................................................. 57
U.S. MEDIA TAKES ON THE WAR ............................................... 59
A SOLDIER IN THE PHILIPPINES ................................................. 61

TRUE VERSION OF THE PHILIPPINE REVOLUTION
by
Don Emilio Aguinaldo y Famy
President of the Philippine Republic.
Tarlak (Philippine Islands),
23rd September, 1899

To
ALL CIVILIZED NATIONS

AND
ESPECIALLY TO THE
GREAT NORTH AMERICAN REPUBLIC

I DEDICATE TO YOU this modest work with a view to informing you respecting the international events which have occurred during the past three years and are still going on in the Philippines, in order that you may be fully acquainted with the facts and be thereby placed in a position to pronounce judgment upon the issue and be satisfied and assured of the Justice which forms the basis and is in fact the foundation of our Cause. I place the simple truth respectfully before and dedicate it to you as an act of homage and as testimony of my admiration for and recognition of the wide knowledge, the brilliant achievements and the great power of other nations, whom I salute, in the name the Philippine nation, with every effusion of my soul.

THE AUTHOR

# I

## The Revolution of 1896

SPAIN MAINTAINED CONTROL of the Philippine Islands for more than three centuries and a half, during which period the tyranny, misconduct and abuses of the Friars and the Civil and Military Administration exhausted the patience of the natives and caused them to make a desperate effort to shake off the unbearable galling yoke on the 26th and 31st August, 1896, then commencing the revolution in the provinces of Manila and Cavite.

On these memorable days the people of Balintawak, Santa Mesa, Kalookan, Kawit, Noveleta and San Francisco de Malabon rose against the Spaniards and proclaimed the Independence of the Philippines, and in the course of the next five days these uprisings were followed by the inhabitants of the other towns in Cavite province joining in the revolt against the Spanish Government although there was no previous arrangement looking to a general revolt. The latter were undoubtedly moved to action by the noble example of the former.

With regard to the rising in the province of Cavite it should be stated that although a call to arms bearing the signatures of Don Augustin Rieta, Don Candido Firona and myself, who were Lieutenants of the Revolutionary Forces, was circulated there was no certainty about the orders being obeyed, or even received by the people, for it happened that one copy of the orders fell into the hands of a Spaniard named Don Fernando Parga, Military Governor of the province, who at that time was exercising the functions of Civil Governor, who promptly reported its contents to the Captain-General of the Philippines, Don Ramon Blanco y Erenas. The latter at once issued orders for the Spanish troops to attack the revolutionary forces.

It would appear beyond doubt that One whom eye of man hath not seen in his wisdom and mercy ordained that the emancipation of the oppressed people of the Philippines should be undertaken at this time, for otherwise it is inexplicable how men armed only with sticks and gulok,[1] wholly unorganized and undisciplined, could defeat the Spanish Regulars in severe engagements at Bakoor, Imus and Noveleta and, in addition to making many of them prisoners, captured a large quantity of arms and ammunition. It was owing to this astonishing success of the revolutionary troops that General Blanco quickly concluded to endeavour, to maintain Spanish control by the adoption of a conciliatory policy under the pretext that thereby he could quel the rebellion, his first act being a declaration to the effect that it was not the purpose of his Government to oppress the people and he had no desire "to slaughter the Filipinos.".

The Government of Madrid disapproved of General Blanco's new policy and speedily appointed Lieutenant-General Don Camilo Polavieja to supersede him, and despatched forthwith a large number of Regulars to the Philippines.

General Polavieja advanced against the revolutionary forces with 16,000 men armed with Mausers, and one field battery. He had scarcely reconquered half of Cavite province when he resigned, owing to bad health. That was in April, 1897.

Polavieja was succeeded by the veteran General Don Fernando Primo de Rivera, who had seen much active service. As soon as Rivera had taken over command of the Forces he personally led his army in the assault upon and pursuit of the revolutionary forces, and so firmly, as well as humanely, was the campaign conducted that he soon reconquered the whole of Cavite province and drove the

---

[1] A kind of sword—*Translator*.

insurgents into the mountains.

Then I established my headquarters in the wild and unexplored mountain fastness of Biak-na-bató, where I formed the Republican Government of the Philippines at the end of May, 1897.

## II

## THE TREATY OF BIAK-NA-BATÓ

DON PEDRO ALEJANDRO PATERNO (who was appointed by the Spanish Governor-General sole mediator in the discussion of the terms of peace) visited Biak-na-bató several times to negotiate terms of the Treaty, which, after negotiations extending over five months, and careful consideration had been given to each clause, was finally completed and signed on the 14th December, 1897, the following being the principal conditions:—

(1) That I would, and any of my associates who desired to go with me, be free to live in any foreign country. Having fixed upon Hongkong as my place of residence, it was agreed that payment of the indemnity of $800,000 (Mexican) should be made in three installments, namely, $400,000 when all the arms in Biak-na-bató were delivered to the Spanish authorities; $200,000 when the arms surrendered amounted to eight hundred stand; the final payment to be made when one thousand stand of arms shall have been handed over to the authorities and the *Te Deum* sung in the Cathedral in Manila as thanksgiving for the restoration of peace. The latter part of February was fixed as the limit of time wherein the surrender of arms should be completed.

(2) The whole of the money was to be paid to me personally, leaving the disposal of the money to my discretion and knowledge of the understanding with my associates and other insurgents.

(3) Prior to evacuating Biak-na-bató the remainder of the insurgent forces under Captain-General Primo de Rivera should send to Biak-na-bató two Generals of the Spanish Army to be held as hostages by my associates who remained there until I and a few of my compatriots arrived in Hongkong and the first installment of the money payment (namely, four hundred thousand dollars) was paid to me.

(4) It was also agreed that the religious corporations in the Philippines be expelled and an autonomous system of government, political and administrative, be established, though by special request of General Primo de Rivera these conditions were not insisted on in the drawing up of the Treaty, the General contending that such concessions would subject the Spanish Government to severe criticism and even ridicule.

General Primo de Rivera paid the first installment of $400,000 while the two Generals were held as hostages in Biak-na-bató.

We, the revolutionaries, discharged our obligation to surrender our arms, which were over 1,000 stand, as everybody knows, it having been published in the Manila newspapers. But the Captain General Primo de Rivera failed to fulfill the agreement as faithfully as we did. The other installments were never paid; the Friars were neither restricted in their acts of tyranny and oppression nor were any steps taken to expel them or secularize the religious Orders; the reforms demanded were not inaugurated, though the *Te Deum* was sung. This failure of the Spanish authorities to abide by the terms of the Treaty caused me and my companions much unhappiness, which quickly changed to exasperation when I received a letter from Lieutenant-Colonel Don Miguel Primo de Rivera (nephew and private Secretary of the above-named General) informing me that I and my companions could never return to Manila.

Was the procedure of this special representative of Spain just?

## III

## NEGOTIATIONS

BUT I AND MY COMPANIONS were not to be kept long in our distress, grieving over the bad faith of the Spaniards, for in the month of March of the year referred to (1898) some people came to me and in the name of the Commander of the U.S.S. Petrel asked for a conference in compliance with the wishes of Admiral Dewey.

I had some interviews with the above-mentioned Commander, *i.e.*, during the evening of the 16th March and 6th April, during which the Commander urged me to return to the Philippines to renew hostilities against the Spaniards with the object of gaining our independence, and he assured me of the assistance of the United States in the event of war between the United States and Spain.

I then asked the Commander of the Petrel what the United States could concede to the Filipinos. In reply he said: *"The United States is a great and rich nation and needs no colonies."*

In view of this reply I suggested to the Commander the advisability of stating in writing what would be agreed to by the United States, and he replied that he would refer the matter to Admiral Dewey.

In the midst of my negotiations with the Commander of the *Petrel* I was interrupted by letters from Isabelo Artacho and his solicitors, on the 5th April, claiming $200,000 of the money received from the Spanish authorities, and asserting that he (Artacho) should receive this sum as salary due to him while acting as Secretary of the Interior, he having been, it was alleged, a member of the Filipino Government established in Biak-na-bató. These letters contained the threat that failure to comply with the demand of Artacho would result in him bringing me before the Courts of Law in Hongkong. It may make the matter clearer if I mention at this point that Isabelo Artacho arrived at Biak-na-bató and made himself known to and mixed with the officers in the revolutionary camp on the 21st day of September, 1897, and was appointed Secretary of the Interior in the early part of November of that year, when the Treaty of Peace proposed and negotiated by Don Pedro Alejandro Paterno was almost concluded, as is proved by the fact that the document was signed on the 14th of December of that year.

In the light of these facts the unjust and unreasonable nature of the claim of Artacho is easily discernable, for it is monstrous to claim $200,000 for services rendered to the Revolutionary Government during such a brief period.

Moreover, it is a fact that it was agreed between ourselves (the leaders of the Revolution assembled in Biak-na-bató) that in the event of the Spaniards failing to comply with each and every one of the terms and conditions of the Agreement the money obtained from the Spanish Government should not be divided, but must be employed in the purchase of arms and ammunition to renew the war of independence.

It is therefore evident that Artacho, in making this preposterous demand, was acting as a spy for the enemy, as an agent of General Primo de Rivera, for he wanted to extinguish the rebellion by depriving its organizers and leaders of the most indispensable element, the "sinews of war," which is money. This was the view, too, of the whole of my colleagues, and it was resolved by us that I should leave Hongkong immediately and thereby avoid the litigation which Artacho seemed bent upon and thereby afford my companions time and opportunity to remove this new and wholly unexpected barrier to the realization of our cherished plans for the emancipation of our beloved fatherland. I am profoundly pleased to say that they succeeded, Artacho withdrawing the suit through a transaction.

In accordance with the decision of the meeting above

referred to, I left Hongkong quietly on the 7th April, 1898, on board the steamship *Taisany*, and after calling at Saigon I reached Singapore as a passenger by the s.s. *Eridan*, landing there as secretly as possible on the 21st April. I at once proceeded to the residence of one of my countrymen.

Thus is explained the cause of the interruption of the vitally important negotiations with Admiral Dewey, initiated by the Commander of the *Petrel*.

But "Man proposes and God disposes" is a proverb which was verified in its fullest sense on this occasion, for, notwithstanding the precautions taken in my journey to avoid identification yet at 4 o'clock in the afternoon of the day I arrived at Singapore an Englishman came to the house in which I was residing and in a cautious manner stated that the United States Consul at that port, Mr. Spencer Pratt, wished to have an interview with Don Emilio Aguinaldo. The visitor was told that in that house they did not know Aguinaldo; this being the prearranged answer for any callers.

But the Englishman returned to the house several times and persisted in saying that it was no use trying to conceal the fact of Aguinaldo's arrival for Consul Pratt had received notice from Admiral Dewey of General Aguinaldo's journey to Singapore.

In reply, the Consul said he would telegraph about this matter to Admiral Dewey, who was, he said, Commander-in-Chief of the squadron which would invade the Philippines, and who had, he also stated, full powers conferred on him by President McKinley.

Between 10 or 12 in the forenoon of the next day the conference was renewed and Mr. Pratt then informed me that the Admiral had sent him a telegram in reply to the wish I had expressed for an agreement in writing. He said the Admiral's reply was—*That the United States would at least recognize the Independence of the Philippines under the protection of the United States Navy. The Consul added that there was no necessity for entering into a formal written agreement because the word of the Admiral and of the United States Consul were in fact equivalent to the most solemn pledge that their verbal promises and assurance would be fulfilled to the letter and were not to be classed with Spanish promises or Spanish ideas of a man's word of honour. In conclusion the Consul said, "The Government of North America, is a very honest, just, and powerful government."*

Being informed of what had been said by the visitor I consented to meet Consul Pratt, and had a strictly private interview with him between 9 and 12 p.m. on 22nd April, 1898, in one of the suburbs of Singapore. As soon as Mr. Pratt met me he said that war had been formally declared by the United States against Spain the day before, i.e., on the 21st April.

In the course of the interview alluded to, Consul Pratt told me that as the Spaniards had not fulfilled the promises made in the Biak-na-bató Agreement, the Filipinos had the right to continue the revolution which had been checked by the Biak-na-bató arrangement, and after urging me to resume hostilities against the Spaniards he assured me that the United States would grant much greater liberty and more material benefits to the Filipinos than the Spaniards ever promised.

I then asked the Consul what benefits the United States would confer on the Philippines, pointing out at the same time the advisability of making an agreement and setting out all the terms and conditions in black and white.

Being as anxious to be in the Philippines as Admiral Dewey and the North American Consul—to renew the struggle for our Independence—I took the opportunity afforded me by these representatives of the United States, and, placing the fullest confidence in their word of honour, I said to Mr. Pratt (in response to his persistent professions of solicitude for the welfare of my countrymen) that he could count upon me when I returned to the Philippines to raise the people as one man against the Spaniards, with the one grand object in view as above mentioned, if I could take firearms with me to distribute amongst my countrymen. I assured him that I would put forth my utmost endeavours to crush and extinguish the power of Spain in the islands and I added that if in possession of one battery of a dozen field-guns I would make the Spaniards surrender Manila in about two weeks.

The Consul said he would help me to get over to the Philippines the consignment of arms in respect of which I had made the preliminary arrangements in Hongkong, and he added that he would at once telegraph to Admiral Dewey informing him of this promise in order that the Admiral might give what assistance laid in his power to make the expedition in question a success.

On the 25th April the last conference was held in the United States Consulate at Singapore. I was invited by the Consul to meet him on this occasion and as soon as we met he said he had received a telegram from the Admiral requesting him to ask me to proceed to Hongkong by first steamer to join the Admiral who was then with his squadron in Mir's Bay; a Chinese harbour close to Hongkong. I replied to this proposal in the affirmative, and gave directions to my *aide-de-camp* to at once procure passages for myself and companions, care being taken that the tickets should bear the assumed names we had adopted on the occasion of our journey from Hongkong to Singapore, it being advisable that we should continue to travel *incognito*.

On the 26th April I called on Consul Pratt to bid him adieu on the eve of my departure from Singapore by the steamship *Malacca*. The Consul, after telling me that when I got near the port of Hongkong I would be met by the Admiral's launch and taken from the *Malacca* to the American squadron (a precaution against news of my movements becoming public property, of which I highly approved), then asked me to appoint him Representative of the Philippines in the United States, there to zealously advocate official recognition of our Independence. My answer was, that I would propose him for the position of Representative of the Philippines in the United States when the Philippine Government was properly organized, though I thought it an insignificant reward for his assistance, for, in the event of our Independence becoming un *fait accompli* I intended to offer him a high position in the Customs Department, besides granting certain commercial advantages and contributing towards the cost of the war whatever sum he might consider due to his Government; because the Filipinos had already decided such a policy was the natural outcome of the exigencies of the situation and could be construed only as a right and proper token of the nation's gratitude.

But to continue the statement of facts respecting my return to Hongkong from Singapore: I left Singapore with my A.D. Cs., Sres Pilar and Leyba, bound for Hongkong by the s.s. *Malacca*, arriving at Hongkong at 2 a.m. on the 1st May, without seeing or hearing anything of the launch which I had been led by Consul Pratt to expect to meet me near the entrance of Hongkong harbour. In response to an invitation from Mr. Rounsevelle Wildman, United States Consul at Hongkong, I wended my way to the United States Consulate and between 9 and 11 p.m. of the same day I had an interview with him. Mr. Wildman told me that Admiral Dewey left for Manila hurriedly in accordance with imperative orders from his Government directing him to attack the Spanish Fleet. He was therefore unable to await my arrival before weighing anchor and going forth to give battle to the Spaniards. Mr. Wildman added that Admiral Dewey left word with him that he would send a gunboat to take me across to the Philippines. In the course of this interview with Mr. Wildman I spoke to him about the shipment of arms to the islands which I had previously planned with him, and it was then agreed among ourselves that he (Mr. Rounsevelle Wildman) and the Filipino Mr. Teodoro Sandico should complete the arrangements for the despatch of the expedition, and I there and then handed to and deposited with them the sum of $50,000.

A steam launch was quickly purchased for $15,000, while

a contract was made and entered into for the purchase of 2,000 rifles at $7 each and 200,000 rounds of ammunition at $33 and 56/100 per 1000.

A week later (7th May) the American despatch-boat *McCulloch* arrived from Manila bringing news of Admiral Dewey's victory over the Spanish fleet, but did not bring orders to convey me to Manila. At 9 o'clock that night I had another interview with Consul Wildman, at his request.

On the 15th of the same month the *McCulloch* again arrived at Hongkong from Manila, this time bringing orders to convey me and my companions to Manila. I was promptly notified of this by Consul Wildman who requested that we go on board the *McCulloch* at 10 o'clock at night on 16th May. Accompanied by Consul Wildman, the Captain of the *McCulloch*, and Mr. John Barrett (who then usually styled himself "ex-Secretary of the United States Legation in Siam") we boarded an American steam launch and proceeded to Chinese Kowloon Bay, where the *McCulloch* was anchored. While bidding us adieu Mr. Barrett said he would call on me in the Philippines, which he did later on in Cavite and Malolos.

Mr. Wildman strongly advised me to establish a Dictatorship as soon as I arrived in the Philippines, and he assured me that he would use his best endeavours to have the arms already contracted for delivered to me in the Philippines, which he in fact did. [It is to be observed, though, that the first expedition having been conducted satisfactorily, the arms reaching me in due course, I was naturally grateful and had confidence in the sincerity and good faith of Consul Wildman, and there was nothing surprising therefore in the fact that I asked him to fit out another expedition and caused the sum of $67,000 to be deposited with him for that purpose. I regret to state, however, that Mr. Wildman has failed to comply with my request and I am informed that he refuses to refund the money.]

The *McCulloch* left Hongkong at 11 a.m. on the 17th May

and arrived off Cavite (Manila Bay) between noon and 1 p.m. on the 19th idem. No sooner had the *McCulloch* dropped anchor than the Admiral's launch, carrying his Adjutant and Private Secretary, came alongside to convey me to the flagship *Olympia*, where I was received with my Adjutant (Sr. Leyba) with the honours due to a General.

The Admiral ushered me into his private quarters, and after the exchange of the usual greetings I asked *whether it was true that he had sent all the telegrams to the Consul at Singapore, Mr. Pratt, which that gentleman had told me he received in regard to myself. The Admiral replied in the affirmative, adding that the United States had come to the Philippines to protect the natives and free them from the yoke of Spain. He said, moreover, that America is exceedingly well off as regards territory, revenue, and resources and therefore needs no colonies, assuring me finally that there was no occasion for me to entertain any doubts whatever about the recognition of the Independence of the Philippines by the United States.* Then Admiral Dewey asked me if I could induce the people to rise against the Spaniards and make a short, sharp, and decisive campaign of it.

I said in reply that events would speak for themselves, but while a certain arms expedition (respecting which Consul Wildman was duly informed that it would be despatched from a Chinese port) was delayed in China we could do nothing, because without arms every victory would assuredly cost us the lives of many brave and dashing Filipino warriors. The Admiral thereupon offered to despatch a steamer to hurry up the expedition. (This, be it borne in mind, in addition to the General orders he had given the Consul to assist us to procure arms and ammunition.) Then he at once placed at my disposal all the guns seized onboard the Spanish warships as well as 62 Mausers and a good many rounds of ammunition which had been brought up from Corregidor Island by the U.S.S. *Petrel*.

I then availed myself of an early opportunity to express

to the Admiral my deep gratitude for the assistance rendered to the people of the Philippines by the United States, as well as my unbounded admiration of the grandeur and beneficence of the American people. I also candidly informed the Admiral that before I left Hongkong the Filipinos residing in that colony held a meeting at which the following question was fully discussed, namely, *the possibility that after the Spaniards were defeated, and their power and prestige in the islands destroyed, the Filipinos might have to wage war against the United States owing to the American Government declining to recognize our independence. In that event the Americans, it was generally agreed, would be sure to defeat us for they would find us worn out and short of ammunition owing to our struggle with the Spaniards. I concluded by asking the gallant Admiral to excuse me for an amount of frankness that might appear to border on impudence, and assured him of the fact that I was actuated only by a desire to have a perfectly clear understanding in the interest of both parties.*

*The Admiral said he was very glad to have this evidence of our earnestness and straightforwardness and he thought the Filipinos and Americans should act towards one another as friends and allies, and therefore it was right and proper that all doubts should be expressed frankly in order that explanations be made, difficulties avoided, and distrust removed; adding that, as he had already indicated,* THE UNITED STATES WOULD UNQUESTIONABLY RECOGNIZE THE INDEPENDENCE OF THE PEOPLE OF THE PHILIPPINES, GUARANTEED AS IT WAS BY THE WORD OF HONOUR OF AMERICANS, *which, he said, is more positive, more irrevocable than any written agreement, which might not be regarded as binding when there is an intention or desire to repudiate it, as was the case in respect of the compact made with the Spaniards at Biak-na-bató. Then the Admiral advised me to at once have made a Filipino National Flag, which he said he would recognize and protect in the presence of the other nations represented by the various squadrons anchored in Manila Bay, adding, however, that he thought it advisable that we should destroy the power of Spain before hoisting our national flag, in order that the act would appear more important and creditable in the eyes of the world and of the United States in particular. Then when the Filipino vessels passed to and fro with the national flag fluttering in the breeze they would attract more attention and be more likely to induce respect for the national colours.*

I again thanked the Admiral for his good advice and generous offers, giving him to understand clearly that I was willing to sacrifice my own life if he would be thereby more exalted in the estimation of the United States, more honoured by his fellow-countrymen.

I added that under the present conditions of hearty co-operation, good fellowship and a clear understanding the whole nation would respond to the call to arms to shake off the yoke of Spain and obtain their freedom by destroying the power of Spain in all parts of the archipelago. If, however, all did not at once join in the movement that should not cause surprise, for there would be many unable to assist owing to lack of arms and ammunition, while others, again, might be reluctant to take an active part in the campaign on account of the loss and inconvenience to themselves and families that would result, from open hostility to the Spaniards.

Thus ended my first interview with Admiral Dewey, to whom I signified my intention to reside for a while at the headquarters of the Naval Commandant of Cavite Arsenal.

## IV

## THE REVOLUTION OF 1898

I RETURNED TO THE *MCCULLOCH* to give directions for the landing of the luggage and *war materials* which I brought over with me from Hongkong. On my way to the *McCulloch* I met several of my old associates in the 1896 revolution who had come over from Bataan province. To these friends I gave two letters directing the people of that province and Zambales to rise against the Spaniards and vigorously attack them.

Before returning to the Arsenal and when near the landing place I came across several bancas [large open boats] loaded with revolutionists of Kawit (my birth-place) who told me they had been looking out for me for about two weeks, the Americans having announced that I would soon return to the islands. The feeling of joy which I experienced on the occasion of this reunion with my own kith and kin—people who had stood shoulder to shoulder with me in the desperate struggles of the 1896–97 revolution—is simply indescribable. Words fail to express my feelings—joy mingled with sadness and strong determination to accomplish the salvation, the emancipation, of my beloved countrymen. Hardly had I set foot in the Naval Headquarters at Cavite, at 4 o'clock in the afternoon, than I availed myself of the opportunity to give these faithful adherents orders similar to those despatched to Bataan and Zambales.

I was engaged the whole of that night with my companions drawing up orders and circulars for the above mentioned purpose.

We were also kept very busy replying to letters which were pouring in from all sides asking for news respecting the reported return of myself to the islands and requesting definite instructions regarding a renewal of hostilities against the Spaniards.

That the invisible, albeit irresistible, hand of Providence was guiding every movement and beneficently favouring all efforts to rid the country of the detestable foreign yoke is fairly evidenced by the rapid sequence of events above recorded, for in no other way can one account for the wonderful celebrity with which news of my projected return spread far and wide.

Sixty-two Volunteers, organized and armed by the Spaniards with Mausers and Remingtons, from San Roque and Caridad, placed themselves under my orders. At first the Americans apprehended some danger from the presence of this armed force, which was promptly placed on guard at the entrance to the Arsenal. When I heard of this I went down and gave them orders to occupy Dalajican, thereby preventing the Spaniards from carrying out their intention to approach Cavite by that route.

When the Americans were informed of what I had done they were reassured, and orders were given to the Captain of the *Petrel* to hand over to me the 62 rifles and ammunition which Admiral Dewey had kindly promised. About 10 a.m. the *Petrel's* launch landed the arms and ammunition in question at the Arsenal and no time was lost in distributing the arms among the men who were by this time coming in ever increasing numbers to offer their services to me and expressing their willingness to be armed and assigned for duty at the outposts and on the firing line.

During the evening of the 20th May the old Revolutionary officer Sr. Luciano San Miguel (now a General in command of a Brigade) came to me and asked for orders, which were given to him to effect the uprising of the provinces of Manila, Laguna, Batangas, Tayabas, Bulakan, Morong, Pampanga, Tarlak, Newva Ecija and other northern provinces. He left the same night to execute the orders.

During the 21st, 22nd and 23rd and subsequent days of that month my headquarters were simply besieged by my countrymen, who poured into Cavite from all sides to offer their services in the impending struggle with the Spaniards. To such an extent, indeed, were my quarters in the Arsenal invaded that I soon found it necessary to repair to another house in the town, leaving the place entirely at the disposal of the U.S. Marines, who were then in charge of and guarding Cavite Arsenal.

V

## The Dictatorial Government

ON THE 24TH MAY a Dictatorial Government was established, my first proclamation being issued that day announcing the system of government then adopted and stating that I had assumed the duties and responsibilities of head of such government. Several copies of this proclamation were delivered to Admiral Dewey and through the favour of his good offices forwarded to the representatives of the Foreign Powers then residing in Manila, notwithstanding our lack of intercourse with Manila.

A few days later the Dictatorial Government was removed to the house formerly occupied by the Spanish Civil Governor of Cavite, because, owing to the great number of visitors from the provinces and the rapid increase of work the accommodation in the private house was wholly inadequate and too cramped. It was while quartered in the first mentioned house that glad tidings reached me of the arrival at Cavite of the long-expected arms expedition. The whole cargo, consisting of 1,999 rifles and 200,000 rounds of ammunition, besides other special munitions of war, was landed at the very same dock of the Arsenal, and was witnessed by the U.S.S. "*Petrel.*"

I immediately despatched a Commission to convey to the Admiral my thanks for the trouble he had taken in sending to hurry up the expedition. I also caused my Commissioners to inform the Admiral that I had fixed the 31st May as the day when the Revolutionary Forces should make a General attack upon the Spaniards. The Admiral returned the compliment by sending his Secretary to congratulate me and my Government upon the activity and enthusiasm displayed in preparing for the campaign, but he suggested that it was advisable to postpone the opening of the campaign to a later date in order that the insurgent troops might be better organized and better drilled. I replied to the Admiral through his Secretary that there was no cause for any anxiety for everything would be in perfect readiness by the 31st and, moreover, that the Filipinos were very anxious to free themselves from the galling Spanish yoke, that they would therefore fight and my troops would make up for any deficiency in discipline by a display of fearlessness and determination to defeat the common enemy which would go far to ensure success, I was, I added, nevertheless profoundly grateful to the Admiral for his friendly advice.

I promptly gave orders for the distribution of the arms which had just arrived, sending some to various provinces and reserving the remainder for the revolutionaries of Kawit, the latter being smuggled into the district of Alapang during the night of 27th May.

## VI

## THE FIRST TRIUMPHS

THE NEXT DAY (8th May, 1898), just when we were distributing arms to the revolutionists of Kawit, in the above mentioned district a column, composed of over 270 Spanish Naval Infantry, appeared in sight. They were sent out by the Spanish General, Sr. Peña, for the purpose of seizing the said consignment of arms.

Then it was that the first engagement of the Revolution of 1898 (which may be rightly styled a continuation of the campaign of 1896–97) took place. The battle raged from 10 a.m. to 3 p.m., when the Spaniards ran out of ammunition and surrendered, with all their arms, to the Filipino Revolutionists, who took their prisoners to Cavite. In commemoration of this glorious achievement I hoisted our national flag in presence of a great crowd, who greeted it with tremendous applause and loud, spontaneous and prolonged cheers for "Independent Philippines" and for "the generous nation"—the United States of America. Several officers and Marines from the American fleet who witnessed the ceremony evinced sympathy with the Filipino cause by joining in the natural and popular rejoicings of the people.

This glorious triumph was merely the prelude to a

succession of brilliant victories, and when the 31st May came—the date fixed for general uprising of the whole of the Philippines—the people rose as one man to crush the power of Spain.

The second triumph was effected in Binakayan, at a place known as *Polvorin*, where the Spanish garrison consisting of about 250 men was attacked by our raw levvies and surrendered in a few hours, their stock of ammunition being completely exhausted.

I again availed myself of the opportunity to hoist our national flag and did so from an upper story of the *Polvorin* facing the sea, with the object of causing the sacred insignia of our Liberty and Independence to be seen fluttering in the breeze by the warships, representing all the great and civilized nations of the world, which were congregated in the harbour observing the providential evolution going on in the Philippines after upwards of three hundred years of Spanish domination.

Scarcely had another hour elapsed before another flag was seen flying over the steeple of the Church at Bakoor—which is also in full view of vessels in the harbour—being the signal of another triumph of our troops over the Spanish forces which held that town. The garrison consisted of about 300 men, who surrendered to the Revolutionary Army when their ammunition was exhausted.

And so the Revolution progressed, triumph following triumph in quick succession, evidencing the power, resolution and ability of the inhabitants of the Philippines to rid themselves of any foreign yoke and exist as an independent State, as I affirmed to Admiral Dewey and in respect of which he and several American Commanders and officers warmly congratulated me, specially mentioning the undeniable triumphs of the Philippine Army as demonstrated and proved by the great number of prisoners we brought into Cavite from all parts of Luzon.

## VII

### The Philippine Flag

IN CONFORMITY WITH MY ORDERS issued on the 1st of September, all Philippine vessels hoisted the national flag, the Marines of the Filipino flotilla being the first to execute that order. Our little flotilla consisted of some eight Spanish steam launches (which had been captured) and five vessels of greater dimensions, namely, the *Taaleño, Baldyan, Taal, Bulucan,* and *Purisima Concepcion.* These vessels were presented to the Philippine Government by their native owners and were converted by us, at our Arsenal, into gunboats, 8 and 9 centimetre guns, taken from the *sunken Spanish warships,* being mounted on board.

Ah! what a beautiful, inspiring joyous sight that flag was fluttering in the breeze from the topmasts of our vessels, side by side, as it were, with the ensigns of other and greater nations, among whose mighty warships our little cruisers passed to and fro dipping their colours, the ensign of Liberty and Independence! With what reverence and adoration it was viewed as it suddenly rose in its stately loneliness crowning our victories, and, as it were, smiling approvingly upon the undisciplined Philippine Army in the moment of its triumphs over the regular forces of the Spanish Government! One's heart swells and throbs again with the emotions of extreme delight; the soul is filled with pride, and the goal of patriotism seems well-nigh reached in the midst of such a magnificent spectacle!

At the end of June I called on Admiral Dewey, who, after complimenting me on *the rapid triumphs of the Philippine Revolution,* told me he had been asked by the German and French Admirals why he allowed the Filipinos to display on their vessels a flag that was not recognized. Admiral Dewey said his reply to the French and German Admirals was—

with *his knowledge and consent the Filipinos used that flag*, and, apart from this, he was of opinion that in view of the courage and steadfastness of purpose displayed in the war against the Spaniards the Filipinos deserved the right to use their flag.

I thereupon expressed to the Admiral my unbounded gratitude for such unequivocal protection, and on returning to the shore immediately ordered the Philippine flotilla to convey troops to the other provinces of Luzon and to the Southern islands, to wage war against the Spaniards who garrisoned them.

## VIII

### EXPEDITION TO BISAYAS

THE EXPEDITION TO BISAYAS was a complete success as far as the conveyance of our troops to the chief strategic points was concerned, our steamers returning safely to Cavite after landing the soldiers. The steamer *Bulusan*, however, which sailed for Masbate with Colonel Sr. Mariano Riego de Dios' column destined for duty in Samar was sighted by the Spanish gunboats *Elcano* and *Uranus*, which gave chase, and the former proving the faster overtook and attacked the *Bulusan* doing so much damage to her that she foundered after a hot engagement in which considerable damage was done to the Spaniard. Happily the crew and troops on board of the *Bulusan* saved their lives by swimming ashore.

## IX

### THE STEAMER "COMPANIA DE FILIPINAS"

IN A FEW DAYS the Spanish steamer *Compania de Filipinas*

was brought to Cavite by my countrymen, who captured her in the harbour of Aparri. Cannon were at once mounted on board this vessel and she was loaded with troops and despatched for Olongapo, but she had not gone far before I sent another gunboat to recall her because Admiral Dewey requested me to do so in order that a question raised by the French Consul might be duly settled. The Admiral having been informed that when captured the *Compania de Filipinas* was flying the Spanish flag abstained from interfering in the matter and handed the French Consul's protest over to me, affirming at the same time that *he and his forces were in no way concerned in the matter.*

This incident, which was soon settled, clearly demonstrates the recognition of and protection extended to the Philippine Revolution by Admiral Dewey.

The *Filipinas* (as this steamer has since been styled) was again despatched to Olongapo and on her way back landed troops in the provinces of Cagayan and the Batanes islands for the purpose of wresting the government of those districts from Spain. This steamer, whose name has more recently been changed to *Luzon*, is at present ashore in the Rio Grande, in Cagayan, where she was beached owing to some damage to her machinery.

When our steamers were leaving the harbour with troops for the provinces they dipped their ensigns in passing Admiral Dewey's flagship *Olympia*, performing this act in conformity with the rules of international courtesy, a demonstration of friendship that was invariably promptly responded to in the usual way.

## X

### The Proclamation of Independence

THE DICTATORIAL GOVERNMENT decided that the

proclamation of Independence should take place on the 12th June, the ceremony in connection therewith to be held in the town of Kawit. With this object in view I sent a Commission to inform the Admiral of the arrangement and invite him to be present on the occasion of the formal proclamation of Independence, a ceremony which was solemnly and impressively conducted. The Admiral sent his Secretary to excuse him from taking part in the proceedings, stating the day fixed for the ceremony was mail day.

About the end of that month (June) the Spanish gunboat *Leyte* escaped from the Macabebe river and reached Manila Bay, where she was seized by General Torres' troops. She had on board part of the troops and volunteers which were under the command of the Filipino Colonel Sr. Eugenio Blanco, but on being sighted by an American gunboat she voluntarily surrendered. Admiral Dewey delivered to me all the prisoners and arms on board the vessel, which latter, however, he took possession of; but after the fall of Manila he demanded that I should give back the prisoners to him.

On the 4th July the first United States military expedition arrived, under command of General Anderson, and it was quartered in Cavite Arsenal. This distinguished General called on me in the Filipino Government House at Cavite, an honour and courtesy which I promptly returned, as was right and proper, seeing that we were friends, of equal rank, and allies. In the course of official intercourse General Anderson solemnly and completely endorsed the promises made by Admiral Dewey to me, asserting on his word of honour that America had not come to the Philippines to wage war against the natives nor to conquer and retain territory, but only to liberate the people from the oppression of the Spanish Government.

A few days before the arrival of this military expedition, and others that followed under command of General Merritt, Admiral Dewey sent his Secretary to my Government to ask me to grant permission for the stationing of American troops in Tambo and Maytubig, Paranaque and Pasay. In view of the important promises of Admiral Dewey, above mentioned, the Dictatorial Government consented to the movement of troops as proposed.

During that month (July) Admiral Dewey accompanied by General Anderson visited Cavite, and after the usual exchange of courtesies he said—"You have had ocular demonstration and confirmation of all I have told you and promised you. How pretty your flag is! It has a triangle, and is something like the Cubans'. Will you give me one as a memento when I go back home?"

I replied that I was fully satisfied with his word of honour and of the needlessness of having our agreement in documentary form. As to the flag he wanted, he could have one whenever he wished.

The Admiral continued: *Documents are useless when there is no sense of honour on one side, as was the case in respect of the compact with the Spaniards, who failed to act up to what had been written and signed. Have faith in my word, and I assure you that the United States will recognize the independence of the country. But I recommend you to keep a good deal of what we have said and agreed secret at present. I further request you to have patience if any of our soldiers insult any Filipinos, for being Volunteers they are as yet undisciplined.*

I replied that I would bear in mind all his advice regarding cautiousness, and that with respect to the misconduct of the soldiers orders had already been issued enjoining forbearance, and I passed the same remarks to the Admiral about unpleasantness possibly arising through lack of discipline of our own forces.

XI

THE SPANISH COMMISSION

AT THIS JUNCTURE the Admiral suddenly changed the

topic of conversation and asked—"Why don't the people in Manila rise against the Spaniards as their countrymen in the provinces have done? Is it true that they accept the *autonomy* offered by General Augustin with a representative Assembly? Is the report which has reached me true, that a Filipino Commission has been sent from Manila to propose to you the acceptance of that *autonomy* coupled with a recognition of your rank of General, as well as recognition of the rank held by your companions?"

"The people of Manila," I answered, "are quiet because they have no arms and because as merchants and landlords they fear that their valuable properties and money in the banks will be confiscated by the Spaniards if they rise up and begin burning and destroying the property of others. On this account they had ostensibly accepted *autonomy*, not because that was what they wanted but more as a means of deceiving the Spaniards and being allowed to live in peace; but I am confident that all the Filipinos in Manila are for *independence*, as will be proved the very day our troops capture Manila. At that time I fully expect the people of Manila will join with us in raising loud cheers for the Independence of the Philippines, making fresh demonstrations of loyalty to our Government."

I also told him it was true that a Mixed Commission had arrived and in the name of General Augustin and Archbishop Nozaleda made certain proposals; but they made known to us their intention to adhere to our Cause. The members of the Commission said the Spaniards instructed them to say they came *motu propio*[2] without being formally appointed or 'coached' by the Spanish authorities in what they should say, representing, on the contrary, that they were faithful interpreters of the sentiment of the people of Manila and that they had good reason for believing that if I was willing to accept *autonomy* General Augustin and Archbishop Nozaleda would recognize my rank of General, and that of my companions, would give me the $1,000,000

---

[2] Of their own free will and accord—*Translator*.

indemnity agreed upon at Biak-na-bató and still unpaid, as well as liberal rewards for and salaries to the members of a popular Assembly promises which the Commissioners did not put any faith in, though some of them held the opinion that the money should be accepted because it would reduce the funds of the Spanish Government and also because the money had been wrung from Filipinos. The Commissioners, I added, left after assuring me that the people in Manila would rise against the Spaniards if supplied with arms, and that the best thing I could do was to make an attack on Manila at the places they pointed out as being the weakest parts of the Spanish defense and consequently the easiest to overcome.

I thanked the Commission for their loyalty and straightforwardness, told them they would be given an escort to take them safely back to the Spanish lines, and that when they got back they should inform those who had sent them that they were not received because they were not duly accredited and that even if they had brought credentials according to what they had seen and heard from the Revolutionists Don Emilio Aguinaldo would certainly not consider, much less accept, their proposals respecting autonomy because the Filipino people had sufficient experience to govern themselves, that they are tired of being victimised and subjected to gross abuses by a foreign nation under whose domination they have no wish to continue to live, but rather wish for their *independence*. Therefore the Spaniards might prepare to defend their sovereignty, for the Filipino Army would vigorously assault the city and with unflagging zeal prosecute the siege until Manila was captured.

I also told the Commissioners to tell Archbishop Nozaleda that he was abusing the privileges and authority of his exalted position; that such conduct was at variance with the precepts of His Holiness the Pope, and if he failed to rectify matters I would throw light on the subject in a way which would bring shame and disgrace upon him. I added that I knew he and General Augustin had commissioned four Germans and five Frenchmen to disguise themselves and assassinate me in the vain hope that once I am disposed of the people of the Philippines would calmly submit to the sovereignty of Spain, which was a great mistake, for were I assassinated, the inhabitants of the Philippines would assuredly continue the struggle with greater vigor than ever. Other men would come forward to avenge my death. Lastly I recommended the Commissioners to tell the people in Manila to go on with their trades and industries and be perfectly at ease about our Government, whose actions were guided in the paths of rectitude and justice, and that since there were no more Friars to corrupt the civic virtues, the Filipino Government was now endeavouring to demonstrate its honesty of purpose before the whole world. There was therefore no reason why they should not go on with their business as usual and should not think of leaving Manila and coming into the Camp, where the resources were limited, where already more were employed than was necessary to meet the requirements of the Government and the Army, and where, too, the lack of arms was sorely felt.

The Commissioners asked me what conditions the United States would impose and what benefits they would confer on the Filipinos, to which I replied that is was difficult to answer that question in view of the secret I was in honour bound to keep in respect of the terms of the Agreement, contenting myself by saying that they could learn a good deal by carefully observing the acts, equivalent to the exercise of sovereign rights, of the Dictatorial Government, and especially the occular demonstrations of such rights on the waters of the harbour.

These statements, which were translated by my interpreter, Sr. Leyba, made such an impression on the Admiral that he interrupted, asking—"Why did you reveal our secret?" Do you mean that you do not intend to keep inviolate our well understood silence and watchword?

I said in reply that I had revealed nothing of the secret

connected with him and the Consul.

The Admiral then thanked me for my cautiousness, bid we good-by and left with General Anderson, after requesting me to refrain from assaulting Manila because, he said, they were studying a plan to take the Walled City with their troops, leaving the suburbs for the Filipino forces.

He advised me, nevertheless, to study other plans of taking the city in conjunction with their forces, which I agreed to do.

## XII

### MORE AMERICAN TROOPS

A FEW DAYS LATER American troops arrived, and with them came General Merritt. The Admiral's Secretary and two officers came to the Dictatoriat Government and asked that we allow them to occupy our trenches at Maytubig; from the harbour side of that place right up to the main road, where they would form a continuation of our lines at Pasay and Singalong. This I also agreed to on account of the solemn promises of the Admiral and the trust naturally placed in them owing to the assistance rendered and recognition of our independence.

Ten days after the Americans occupied the trenches at Maytubig (this move being well known by the Spaniards who were entrenched at the Magazine in San Antonio Abad) their outposts, composed of a few men only, were surprised by the Spaniards, who made a night attack on them. They had barely time to get out of their beds and fall back on the centre, abandoning their rifles and six field-guns in their precipitate retreat.

The firing being distinctly heard, our troops immediately rushed to the assistance of our friends and allies, repulsing the Spaniards and recapturing the rifles and field-guns, which I ordered to be returned to the Americans as a token of our good-will and friendship.

General Noriel was opposed to this restitution, alleging that the arms did not belong to the Americans since the Filipino troops captured them from the Spaniards. But I paid no attention to the reasonable opposition of my General and gave imperative instructions that they be returned to the Americans, showing thereby clearly and positively the good-will of the Filipinos. The said rifles and field-guns, with a large quantity of ammunition, was therefore restored to those who were then our allies, notwithstanding the fact of General Noriel's brigade capturing them at a cost of many lives of our compatriots.

Later on more American reinforcements arrived and again Admiral Dewey, through his Secretary, asked for more trenches for their troops, averring that those which we had given up to them before were insufficient. We at once agreed and their lines were then extended up to Pasay.

## XIII

## THE THIRTEENTH OF AUGUST

THE 13TH AUGUST arrived, on which day I noticed a general advance of the American land and sea forces towards Manila, the former being under command of General Anderson at Paranaque.

Subsequently I ordered a general assault of the Spanish lines and in the course of this movement General Pio del Pilar succeeded in advancing through Sampalok and attacked the Spanish troops who where defending the Puente Colgante,[3] causing the enemy to fall back on the Bridge of Spain. The column commanded by our General, Sr. Gregorio II. del Pilar, took the suburbs of Pretil, Tendo,

---

[3] Suspension bridge.—*Translator.*

Divisoria and Paseo de Azcarraga, situated north of Manila city; while General Noriel's command, near Pasay, took the suburbs of Singalong and Pako, and following the American column he out-flanked the Spaniards who were defending San Antonio Abad. The Spanish officers observing General Noriel's move ordered their men to retreat towards the Walled City, whereupon the Americans who held the foremost trenches entered Malate and Ermita without firing a shot. At this point the Americans met General Noriel's troops who had captured the above mentioned suburbs and were quartered in the building formerly used by the Exposicion Regional de Filipinas,[4] in the Normal, and in Sr. Perez' house in Paco.

In Santa Ana (the eastern section of Manila) General Ricarto successfully routed five companies of Spaniards, being aided in this by the manoeuvres of General Pio del Pilar's brigade.

## XIV

### First Clouds

OUR TROOPS SAW the American forces landing on the sea shore near the Luneta and Paseo de Santa Lucia, calling the attention of everybody to the fact that the Spanish soldiers in the city forts were not firing on them (the Americans), a mystery that was cleared up at sunset when details of the capitulation of Manila, by General Jaudenes in accordance with terms of an agreement with General Merritt, became public property—a capitulation which the American Generals reserved for their own benefit and credit in contravention of the agreement arrived at with Admiral Dewey in the arrangement of plans for the final combined

---

[4] 2 Philippine Local Exhibition.—*Translator.*

assault on and capture of Manila by the allied forces, American and Filipino.

Some light was thrown upon this apparently inexplicable conduct of the American Commanders by the telegrams which I received during that day from General Anderson, who wired me from Maitubig asking me to issue orders forbidding our troops to enter Manila, a request which I did not comply with because it was not in conformity with the agreement, and it was, moreover, diametrically opposed to the high ends of the Revolutionary Government, that after going to the trouble of besieging Manila for two months and a half, sacrificing thousands of lives and millions of material interests, it should be supposed such sacrifices were made with any other object in view than the capture of Manila and the Spanish garrison which stubbornly defended the city.

But General Merritt, persistent in his designs, begged me not only through the Admiral but also through Major Bell to withdraw my troops from the suburbs to (as it was argued) prevent the danger of conflict which is always to be looked for in the event of dual military occupation; also by so doing to avoid bringing ridicule upon the American forces; offering, at the same time, in three letters, to negotiate after his wishes were complied with. To this I agreed, though neither immediately nor at one time, but making our troops retire gradually up to the blockhouses in order that the whole of the inhabitants of Manila should witness the proceedings of our troops and amicability toward our American allies.

Up to that time, and in fact right up to the time when the Americans openly commenced hostilities against us, I entertained in my soul strong hopes that the American Commanders would make absolute with their Government the verbal agreement made and entered into with the Leader of the Philippine Revolution, notwithstanding the indications to the contrary which were noticeable in their conduct, especially in respect of the conduct of Admiral Dewey, who, without any reason or justification, one day in the month of October seized all our steamers and launches.

Being informed of this strange proceeding, and at the time when the Revolutionary Government had its headquarters in Malolos, I despatched a Commission to General Otis to discuss the matter with him. General Otis gave the Commissioners a letter of recommendation to the Admiral to whom he referred them; but the Admiral declined to receive the Commission notwithstanding General Otis's recommendation.

Notwithstanding the procedure of the American Commanders, so contrary to the spirit of all the compacts and antecedents above mentioned, I continued to maintain a friendly attitude towards them, sending a Commission to General Merritt to bid him farewell on the eve of his departure for Paris. In his acknowledgement of his courtesy General Merritt was good enough to say that he would advocate the Filipino Cause in the United States. In the same manner I sent to Admiral Dewey a *punal*[5] in a solid silver scabbard and a walking stick of the very best cane with gold handle engraved by the most skilful silversmiths as a souvenir and mark of our friendship. This the Admiral accepted, thereby in some measure relieving my feelings and the anxiety of my compatriots constituting the Revolutionary Government, whose hearts were again filled with pleasant hopes of a complete understanding with Admiral Dewey.

## XV

## Vain Hopes

Vain indeed became these hope when news arrived that Admiral Dewey had acted and was continuing to act against the Revolutionary Government by order of His Excellency Mr. McKinley, who, prompted by the "Imperialist" party,

---

[5] Short sword—*Translator.*

had decided to annex the Philippines, granting, in all probability, concessions to adventurers to exploit the immense natural wealth lying concealed under our virgin soil.

This news was received in the Revolutionary camp like a thunderbolt out of a clear sky. Some cursed the hour and the day we treated verbally with the Americans; some denounced the ceding of the suburbs, while others again were of opinion that a Commission should be sent to General Otis to draw from him clear and positive declarations on the situation, drawing up a treaty of amity and commerce if the United States recognize our independence or at once commence hostilities if the States refused.

In this crisis I advised moderation and prudence, for I still had confidence in the justice and rectitude of United States Congress, which, I believed, would not approve the designs of the Imperialist party and would give heed to the declarations of Admiral Dewey, who, in the capacity of an exalted Representative of the United States in these Islands concerted and covenanted with me and the people of the Philippines recognition of our independence.

In fact in no other way was such a serious matter to be regarded, for if America entrusted to Admiral Dewey the honour of her forces in such a distant region, surely the Filipinos might equally place their trust in the word of honour of such a polished, chivalrous gentleman and brave sailor, in the firm belief, of course, that the great and noble American people would neither reject his decision nor expose to ridicule the illustrious conqueror of the Spanish fleet.

In the same way the not less known and notorious circumstances, that the American Commanders who came soon after the echoes of the Admiral's victory reached their native shores, namely, Generals Merritt, Anderson and Otis, proclaimed to the people of the Philippines that America did not come to conquer territories, but to liberate its inhabitants from the oppression of Spanish Sovereignty. I would therefore also expose to universal ridicule and contempt the honour of these Commanders if the United States, by repudiating their official and public acts, attempts to annex these islands by conquest.

## XVI

### THE AMERICAN COMMISSION

WITH SUCH PRUDENT as well as well founded reflections, I succeeded in calming my companions shortly before the official news arrived reporting that the Washington Government, acting on Admiral Dewey's suggestion, had intimated its intention to despatch a Civil Commission to Manila which would treat with the Filipinos with a view to arriving at a definite understanding respecting the government of the Islands.

Joy and satisfaction now filled the breasts of all the Revolutionists, and I thereupon set about the appointment of a Commission to meet the American Commissioners. At the same time I gave strict orders that the most friendly relations should be maintained with the Americans, enjoining toleration and overlooking of the abuses and atrocities of the soldiery because the effect on the Commissioners would not be good it they found us at loggerheads with their nation's forces.

But the abases of the Americans were now becoming intolerable. In the market-place at Arroceros they killed a woman and a little boy under the pretext that they were surprising a gambling den, thus causing the greatest indignation of a great concourse of people in that vicinity.

My Adjutants, too, who hold passes permitting them to enter Manila with their uniform and sidearms, were molested by being repeatedly stopped by every patrol they met, it, being perfectly evident that, the intention was to irritate them by exposing them to public ridicule.

While this sort of thing was going on as against our people the American Commanders and officers who visited our camp were treated with the utmost courtesy and consideration.

In Lacoste Street an American guard shot and killed a boy seven years of age for taking a banana from a Chinaman.

The searching of houses was carried on just as it was during the Spanish regime, while the American soldiers at the outposts often invaded our lines, thus irritating our sentries. It would make this book a very large volume if I continued to state seriatim the abuses and atrocities committed by the American soldiery in those days of general anxiety.

It seemed as if the abuses were authorised or at least winked at in official quarters for the purpose of provoking an outbreak of hostilities. Excitement ran high among all classes of people, but the Filipino Government, which had assumed responsibility for the acts of the people, by the constant issue of prudent orders succeeded in calming the excited populace and maintained peace, advising all sufferers to be patient and prudent pending the arrival of the Civil Commission.

## XVII

### Impolitic Acts

AT SUCH A CRITICAL JUNCTURE as this, and before the anxiously-awaited Civil Commission arrived, it occurred to General Otis, Commandant of the American forces, to commit two more impolitic acts. One of them was the order to search our telegraph offices in Sagunro Street, in Tondo, where the searching party seized the apparatus and detained the officer in charge, Sr. Reyna, in the Fuerza Santiago[6] under the pretext that he was conspiring against the Americans.

How and why was Sr. Reyna conspiring? Was not this sufficient for the Filipino Government to give the order to attack and rescue Reyna and thereby we (eight thousand strong) be plunged immediately into war with the United States? Was there any reason for conspiring when the power was in our own hands? And, above all, would a telegraphist, be likely to interfere in affaires de guerre when there was an army near by to attend to such matters?

It was abundantly manifest that the object was by wounding the feelings of and belittling the Filipino Government to provoke a collision, and it was clear also that this system of exasperating us was not merely the wanton act of the soldiery but was actually prompted by General Otis himself, who, imbued with imperialistic tendencies, regarded the coming of the Civil Commission with disfavour and especially would it be unsatisfactory that this Commission should find the Philippines in a state of perfect tranquility, because it was evident to the said General, as well as to the whole world, that the Filipinos would assuredly have arrived at a definite amicable agreement with the aforesaid Commission if it reached the islands while peace prevailed.

We, the Filipinos, would have received the Commission with open arms and complete accord as honourable Agents of the great American nation. The Commissioners could have visited all our provinces, seeing and taking note of the complete tranquility throughout our territory. They could have seen our cultivated lands, examined our Constitution and investigated the administration of public affairs in perfect peace and safety, and have felt and enjoyed the inimitable charm of our Oriental style,—half negligent, half solicitude, warmth and chilliness, simple confidence and suspiciousness; characteristics which cause descriptions of

---

[6] The "Black Hole" of Manila.

contact with us to be depicted by foreigners in thousands of different hues.

Ah! but neither did General Otis nor the Imperialists wish for such a landscape. It was better for their criminal designs that the American Commission should view the desolation and horrors of war in the Philippines, inhaling on the very day of their arrival the revolting odour emitted from American and Filipino corpses. It was better for their purposes that that gentleman, Mr. Schurman, President of the Commission, should return from Manila, limiting his investigation to inquiries among the few Filipinos, who, seduced with gold, were siding with the Imperialists. It were better for them that the Commission should view the Philippines problem through fire and slaughter, in the midst of whizzing bullets and the uncontrolled passion of infuriated foes, thus preventing them from forming correct judgment of the exact and natural conditions of the problem. Ah! it was, lastly, better that the Commission return to the States defeated in its mission of obtaining peace and blaming me and other Filipinos for its inability to settle matters, when, in reality, I and all the Philippine people were longing that that peace had been concluded yesterday,—long before now—but an honest and honourable peace, honourable alike for the United States and the Philippine Republic in order that it be sincere and everlasting.

The second impolitic act of General Otis was the issue of a proclamation on the 4th of January, 1899, asserting in the name of President McKinley the sovereignty of America in these islands, with threats of ruin, death and desolation to all who declined to recognize it.

I, Emilio Aguinaldo—though the humble servant of all, am, as President of the Philippine Republic, charged with the safeguarding of the rights and independence of the people who appointed me to such an exalted position of trust and responsibility—mistrusted for the first time the honour of the Americans, perceiving of course that this proclamation of General Otis completely exceeded the limits of prudence and that therefore no other course was open to me but to repel with arms such unjust and unexpected procedure on the part of the commander of friendly forces.

I protested, therefore, against such a proclamation—also threatening an immediate rupture of friendly relations,—for the whole populace was claiming that an act of treason had been committed, plausibly asserting that the announcement of the Commission applied for by Admiral Dewey was a ruse, and that what General Otis was scheming for was to keep us quiet while he brought reinforcement after reinforcement from the United States for the purpose of crushing our untrained and badly equipped Army with one blow.

But now General Otis acted for the first time like a diplomatist, and wrote me, through his Secretary, Mr. Carman, a letter inviting the Filipino Government to send a Commission to meet an American Commission for the purpose of arriving at an amicable arrangement between both parties; and although I placed no trust in the professions of friendly intentions of the said General—whose determination
to prevent the Commission arriving at a peaceful solution of the difficulties was already evident—I acceded to the request, partly because I saw the order, dated 9th January, given by the above mentioned General confirmed, and on the other hand to show before the whole world my manifest wishes for the conservation of peace and friendship with the United States, solemnly compacted with Admiral Dewey.


## XVIII

## THE MIXED COMMISSION

CONFERENCES OF THE MIXED COMMISSION, Americans and Filipinos, were held in Manila from the 11th to the 31st of the said month of January, the Filipino Commissioners clearly expressing the wish of our people for recognition as an independent nation.

They also frankly stated the complaints of the Filipino people about the abuses and atrocities of the American soldiery, being attentively and benevolently listened to by the American Commissioners. The latter replied that they had no authority to recognize the Filipino Government, their mission being limited to hearing what the Filipinos said, to collect data to formulate the will of our people and transmit it fully and faithfully to the Government of Washington, who alone could arrive at a definite decision on the subject. These conferences ended in perfect harmony, auguring well for happier times and definite peace when Mr. McKinley should reply to General Otis's telegrams transmitting our wishes with his favourable recommendaions, as the American Commissioners said.

## XIX

### Outbreak of Hostilities

WHILE I, THE GOVERNMENT, the Congress and the entire populace were awaiting the arrival of such a greatly desired reply, many fairly overflowing with pleasant thoughts, there came the fatal day of the 4th February, during the night of which day the American forces suddenly attacked all our lines, which were in fact at the time almost deserted, because being Saturday, the day before a regular feast day, our Generals and some of the most prominent officers had obtained leave to pass the Sabbath with their respective families.

General Pantaleon Garcia was the only one who at such a critical moment was at his post in Maypajo, north of Manila, Generals Noriel, Rizal and Ricarte and Colonels San Miguel,

Cailles and others being away enjoying their leave.

General Otis, according to trustworthy information, telegraphed to Washington stating that the Filipinos had attacked the American Army. President McKinley read aloud the telegram in the Senate, where the Treaty of Paris of the 10th December, 1898, was being discussed with a view to its ratification, the question of annexation of the Philippines being the chief subject of debate, and through this criminal procedure secured the acceptation of the said Treaty in toto by a majority of only three votes[7] which were cast simultaneously with a declaration that the voters sided with the "Ayes" on account of war having broken out in these Islands.

This singular comedy could not continue for a great length of time because the Filipinos could never be the aggressors as against the American forces, with whom we had sworn eternal friendship and in whose power we expected to find the necessary protection to enable us to obtain recognition of our independence from the other Powers.

The confusion and obfuscation of the first moments was indeed great, but before long it gave place to the light of Truth which shone forth serene, bringing forth serious reflections.

When sensible people studied the acts of Mr. McKinley, sending reinforcement after reinforcement to Manila at a time after an armistice was agreed upon and even when peace with Spain prevailed; when they took into account that the despatch of the Civil Commission to settle terms of a treaty of amity with the Filipinos was being delayed; when, too, they knew of the antecedents of my alliance with Admiral Dewey, prepared and arranged by the American Consuls of Singapore and Hongkong, Mr. Pratt and Mr. Wildman; when they became acquainted with the actual state of affairs on the 4th February knowing that the

---

[7] Many of the American papers reported that the majority was *one* vote only in excess of the absolutely requisite two-thirds majority.

Filipinos were awaiting the reply of Mr. McKinley to the telegram of General Otis in which he transmitted the peaceful wish of the Filipino people to live as an independent nation; when, lastly, they riveted their attention to the terms of the Treaty of Paris, the approval of which, in as far as it concerned the annexation of the Philippines, was greeted with manifestations of joy and satisfaction by the Imperialist party led by Mr. McKinley, then their eyes were opened to the revelations of truth, clearly perceiving the base, selfish and inhuman policy which Mr. McKinley had followed in his dealings with us the Filipinos, sacrificing remorselessly to their unbridled ambition the honour of Admiral Dewey, exposing this worthy gentleman and illustrious conqueror of the Spanish fleet to universal ridicule; for no other deduction can follow from the fact that about the middle of May of 1898, the U.S.S. *McCulloch* brought me with my revolutionary companions from Hongkong, by order of the above mentioned Admiral, while now actually the United States squadron is engaged in bombarding the towns and ports held by these revolutionists, whose objective is and always has been Liberty and Independence.

The facts as stated are of recent date and must still be fresh in the memory of all.

Those who in May, 1898, admired the courage of Admiral Dewey's sailors and the humanitarianism of this illustrious Commander in granting visible aid to an oppressed people to obtain freedom and independence, surely cannot place an honest construction upon the present inhuman war when contrasting it with those lofty and worthy sentiments.

I need not dwell on the cruelty which, from the time of the commencement of hostilities, has characterized General Otis's treatment of the Filipinos, shooting in secret many who declined to sign a petition asking for autonomy. I need not recapitulate the ruffianly abuses which the American soldiers committed on innocent and defenseless people in Manila, shooting women and children simply because they were leaning out of windows; entering houses at midnight without the occupants' permission—forcing open trunks and wardrobes and stealing money, jewelry and all valuables they came across; breaking chairs, tables and mirrors which they could not carry away with them, because, anyhow, they are consequences of the war, though improper in the case of civilized forces. But what I would not leave unmentioned is the inhuman conduct of that General in his dealings with the Filipino Army, when, to arrange a treaty of peace with the Civil Commission, of which Mr. Schurman was President, I thrice sent emissaries asking for a cessation of hostilities.

General Otis refused the envoys' fair and reasonable request, replying that he would not stop hostilities so long as the Philippine Army declined to lay down their arms.

But why does not this Army deserve some consideration at the hands of General Otis and the American forces? Had they already forgotten the important service the Filipino Army rendered to the Americans in the late war with Spain?

Had General Otis forgotten the favours conferred on him by the Filipino Army, giving up to him and his Army the suburbs and blockhouses which at such great sacrifice to themselves the Filipinos had occupied?

Why should General Otis make such a humiliating condition a prime factor or basis of terms of peace with an Army which stood shoulder to shoulder with the American forces, freely shedding its blood, and whose heroism and courage were extolled by Admiral Dewey and other Americans?

This unexplained conduct of General Otis, so manifestly contrary to the canons of international law and military honour, is eloquent testimony of his deliberate intention to neutralize the effects of Mr. Schurman's pacific mission.

What peace can be concerted by the roaring of cannon and the whizzing of bullets?

What is and has been the course of procedure of General Brooke in Cuba? Are not the Cubans still armed, notwithstanding negotiations for the pacification and future government of that Island are still going on?

Are we, perchance, less deserving of liberty and independence than those revolutionists?

Oh, dear Philippines! Blame your wealth, your beauty for the stupendous disgrace that rests upon your faithful sons.

You have aroused the ambition of the Imperialists and Expansionists of North America and both have placed their sharp claws upon your entrails!

Loved mother, sweet mother, we are here to defend your liberty and independence to the death! We do not want war; on the contrary, we wish for peace; but honourable peace, which does not make you blush nor stain your forehead with shame and confusion. And we swear to you and promise that while America with all her power and wealth could possibly vanquish us; killing all of us; but enslave us, never!!!

No; this humiliation is not the compact I celebrated in Singapore with the American Consul Pratt. This was not the agreement stipulated for with Mr. Wildman, American Consul in Hongkong. Finally, it was not the subjection of my beloved country to a new alien yoke that Admiral Dewey promised me.

It is certain that these three have abandoned me, forgetting that I was sought for and taken from my exile and deportation; forgetting, also, that neither of these three solicited my services in behalf of American Sovereignty, they paying the expense of the Philippine Revolution for which, manifestly, they sought me and brought me back to your beloved bosom!

If there is, as I believe, one God, the root and fountain of all justice and only eternal judge of international disputes, it will not take long, dear mother, to save you from the hands, of your unjust enemies. So I trust in the honour of Admiral Dewey: So I trust in the rectitude of the great people of the United States of America, where, if there are ambitious Imperialists, there are defenders of the humane doctrines of the immortal Monroe, Franklin, and Washington; unless the race of noble citizens, glorious founders of the present greatness of the North American Republic, have so degenerated that their benevolent influence has become subservient to the grasping ambition of the Expansionists, in which latter unfortunate circumstance would not death be preferable to bondage?

Oh, sensible American people! Deep is the admiration of all the Philippine people and of their untrained Army of the courage displayed by your Commanders and soldiers. We are weak in comparison with such Titanic instruments of your Government's ambitious Caesarian policy and find it difficult to effectively resist their courageous onslaught. Limited are our warlike resources, but we will continue this unjust, bloody, and unequal struggle, not for the love of war—which we abhor—but to defend our incontrovertible rights of Liberty and Independence (so dearly won in war with Spain) and our territory which is threatened by the ambitions of a party that is trying to subjugate us.

Distressing, indeed, is war! Its ravages cause us horror. Luckless Filipinos succumb in the confusion of combat, leaving behind them mothers, widows and children. America could put up with all the misfortunes she brings on us without discomfort; but what the North American people are not agreeable to is that she should continue sacrificing her sons, causing distress and anguish to mothers, widows and daughters to satisfy the whim of maintaining a war in contravention of their honourable traditions as enunciated by Washington and Jefferson.

Go back, therefore, North American people, to your old-time liberty. Put your hand on your heart and tell me: Would it be pleasant for you if, in the course of time, North America should find herself in the pitiful plight, of a weak and oppressed people and the Philippines, a free and powerful nation, then at war with your oppressors, asked for your aid promising to deliver you from such a weighty yoke, and after defeating her enemy with your aid she set about subjugating you, refusing the promised liberation?

Civilized nations! Honourable inhabitants of the United States, to whose high and estimable consideration I submit this unpretentious work, herein you have the providential facts which led to the unjust attack upon the existence of the Philippine Republic and the existence of those for whom, though unworthy, God made me the principal guardian.

The veracity of these facts rests upon my word as President of this Republic and on the honour of the whole population of eight million souls, who, for more than three hundred years have been sacrificing the lives and wealth of their brave sons to obtain due recognition of the natural rights of mankind—liberty and independence.

If you will do me the honour to receive and read this work and then pass judgment impartially solemnly declaring on which side right and justice rests, your respectful servant will be eternally grateful.

(Signed) Emilio Aguinaldo. Tarlak, 23rd September, 1899.

# IMAGES OF THE WAR

**Above Left:** Revolutionary President Aquinaldo

**Above Right:** Contemporary *Harper's Weekly* illustration of the Balangiga Massacre. A surprise Filipino guerrillo raid in September, 1901, killed 48 Americans, in America's worst defeat of the war.

**Center:** One of Aguinaldo's most celebrated generals, Gregorio del Pilar (later killed in combat), with his troops.

**Left:** Emilio Aguinaldo arrives aboard the *USS Vicksburg* after his capture, effectively ending the war.

**Top L:** Wounded American soldiers.
**Top R:** Admiral George Dewey, who, as Commodore, led U.S. fleet into Manila Bay.
**Center L:** U.S. troops guard Filipino prisoners.
**Center R and Bottom:** U.S. forces had access to the latest weaponry, while Filipino troops were forced to rely on outdated weaponry left behind by the Spanish.

# U.S. Media Takes on the War

**L:** Cartoon that appeared on a 1902 *Life Magazine* cover. The caption, referring to the group of European generals reads: *Chorus in Background:}* Those pious Yankees can't throw stones at us anymore.

Some U.S. officers in the field adopted a technique learned from minority Filipinos who sided with the Americans. This "water cure" was employed to force civilians and captured troops to reveal inform-ation. It consisted of holding open the victim's mouth and pouring in water until the stomach painfully expanded.

War opponents were outraged at the clear violation of military regu-lations, but no one was severely punished for the offenses.

**Above:** 1902 Political cartoon in the *New York Journal*.

In 1901, in response to the Balangia Massacre, General Jacob H. Smith ordered that no prisoners be taken and that everyone over the age of ten capable of bearing arms be killed. An army officer since the Civil War, Smith had a long history of misconduct, including an 1885 court martial. For this final offense, he was court martialed and forced into retirement.

# A Soldier in the Philippines
by
Needom N. Freeman

# Chapter I

NEEDOM FREEMAN, in the United States regular army during the years 1898–1900, was born in the quiet little country village of Barrettsville, Dawson County, Ga., on the 25th of September, 1874.

Many things have been said and written of army life during the Spanish-American war, but usually from the officers' point of view. As a matter of fact the ideas of a private if spoken or written are unbelieved simply because the prestige of office was not attached, and receives but little credit.

The early part of my life was passed in and near the little village of my birth. Working on the farm and attending the village school a few months during the time when farming operations were suspended, consumed about all my time. My father being a poor man with a large family and unable to give his children the benefit of any advanced education, it fell to my lot to receive but little instruction. I was the eighth child in a family of thirteen—five sons and eight daughters.

Having attained the long awaited age of twenty-one, when most young men are buoyant and full of hope and ambition, I turned my thoughts westward, where I hoped to make my fortune. I gathered together my few possessions and proceeded to Texas, arriving at Alvarado, Texas, the second day of November, 1895.

Obtaining employment on a farm, my old occupation was resumed for eighteen weeks, but finding this too commonplace and not fulfilling my desires nor expectations, the farm work was once more given up.

I obtained a position with a wrecking crew on the Santa

## A Soldier in the Philippines

Fe Railroad. For twelve months I worked with this crew, then gave it up in disgust.

A few weeks' employment in the cotton mills of Dallas, Texas, were sufficient to satisfy me with that sort of work.

I next obtained employment with the street railroad of Dallas, filling the position of motorman, which I held for three months. One night, while with several friends, the subject of enlisting in the army was discussed; this strongly appealed to me, and studying the matter further, I became enthused over the idea. I determined to enlist at once. My position as motorman with the street railroad company was given up. My salary was forty-five dollars a month, as against one-third that amount in the army, but this made little difference to me. I was anxious to be a soldier and live the life of one.

I proceeded to the recruiting office in Dallas to stand an examination, was weighed, then measured all over, every scar was measured, my complexion was noted, my age, place of birth and all about my people were taken. My fingers and toes were twisted and almost pulled off. It occurred to me that possibly my examiners thought my fingers and toes might be artificial. After part of two days' weighing, measuring, finger pulling, toe-twisting and questioning I was pronounced subject and sent to the St. George Hotel, in Dallas, to await further orders. Of twelve applicants who were standing the same examination I was the only successful one. I enlisted under Lieutenant Charles Flammil for a service of three years, unless discharged before the expiration of that time. I was to obey all the orders of my superior officers, which meant every officer from corporal up.

From Dallas I was sent to Fort McIntosh, south-west of Dallas, on the border of Texas and Mexico, on the Rio Grande. My long cherished hope was now being fulfilled. I had from a mere boy had a desire to be one of Uncle Sam's soldiers and fight for my country. I had now entered the service for three years and will let the reader judge for himself whether or not he thinks that I should be satisfied with the service and experience of a soldier.

Fort McIntosh is in Laredo, Texas. Here I was assigned, upon my arrival, to Company A, Twenty-third United States Infantry. I had only been there a few days when Company A was ordered out on a practice march of one hundred and twenty miles. Of course I wanted to go, thinking it would be a picnic. I only had a few days' drilling at the fort, and that was all I ever had, but I was anxious to go on this march with my company, and Goodale, called "Grabby" by the men, had my uniform and necessary equipage issued to me and let me go with the company. I learned during the first days' march its object was not to have a picnic, but just to try us and prepare us for the service we might at any time be called upon to perform. We were to get hardened a little by this practice march.

The second day out we were halted every hour and rested ten minutes. During one of those rests I pulled off my shoes to see what was hurting my feet. I found on each of my heels a large blister and several small ones. A non-commissioned officer saw the condition of my feet and ordered me into the ambulance. I was afraid the soldiers would laugh at me for falling out. First I hesitated, but very soon I had plenty of company in the ambulance.

The march was through a rough country, the roads were very bad, and travel was difficult. Twenty miles a day through chaparral bushes and cactus is a good day's march for soldiers, with all their equipage. The infantryman carried a rifle, belt, haversack and canteen. Tents were pitched every night and guards stationed around the camp to keep away prowling Mexicans and others who would steal the provisions of the camp. Tents were struck at morning and everything put in readiness for the day's march. The company was out fifteen days on that practice march across the plains. Four days, however, were really holidays. We spent them hunting and fishing. Fish and game were plentiful. A few deer were to be found, but ducks and blue quail were the principal game. The

## A Soldier in the Philippines

company returned to Fort McIntosh on the third of December.

I had to be drilled as a recruit; never having had any military training, everything was new to me. I was drilled hard for a month before I was assigned to the company for duty. That month's drill was very hard.

After I was assigned for duty I learned something new about military affairs every day for a year. The manner of all the drill masters was very objectionable to me at first; I did not like the way they spoke to a soldier and gave commands, which, if disobeyed, punishment was inflicted. The month I drilled as a recruit by myself I was under Sergeant Robert Scott of my company. During that time I thought Sergeant Scott the most unkind man I had ever seen. He looked ugly and talked harshly. I thought he meant every word he said. After I learned how the commands were given and was taught how to execute them, it seemed very simple and then I was assigned for duty.

When my time came to serve on guard duty I did not understand the "general orders" and "special orders." I went on guard perfectly bewildered with the instructions given me about my duties.

I did not know what to do. I watched for the officer of the day to make his round and give orders every day and night.

Two hours' duty on post was the time we stood guard before being relieved by the proper authority. If a man is caught sitting down while on duty he is severely punished by being placed in the guard house, and sentenced to hard labor for a long time. Sometimes the labor sentence runs as high as six months or more, according to the gravity of the offense.

I was very careful not to get in the guard house or miss roll call, having to pay fines or working hard all day with a sentry over me.

Every soldier had to be on his bunk at eleven o'clock at night; his check was taken and delivered to the officer of the day. Nine o'clock was bed time, but the checks were not taken up until eleven. The first call of the morning was sounded at a quarter before six, when we must answer to reveille, followed by a drilling exercise of fifteen minutes. After breakfast every soldier had to sweep under his bunk and prepare it and himself for inspection, which took place after drill hour, which was from eight to nine o'clock.

A gymnastic drill of thirty minutes each day, except Saturday and Sunday, was given the company for a month, then for three months this was omitted, then another month's drill was given us, and then the same intermission; thus we had them alternately the whole year.

The Sabbath receives but little notice in the army. All duties went on just as any other day.

Several hours every day were unoccupied by the soldier's duties. The men could amuse themselves during these hours by reading newspapers and books, as a very good library was at hand. Aside from reading were such amusements. as billiards, cards and music. These became monotonous and disgusting to me, and in less than two months I would have gladly given up my position, but I was in for three years, and had to stay and make the best of it.

## Chapter II

THE CHRISTMAS HOLIDAYS were delightful indeed for soldiers, no tasks to perform for one whole week, except guard duty. The week was spent in gambling and revelry.

All other holidays meant hard work all day for soldiers; usually they were days of celebrating some event in the history of our country or some man must be honored, and homage paid to his memory. The soldiers on these occasions had to parade and march along the streets all day. Every holiday, except that of Christmas, was a dreaded day to soldiers.

April first, 1898, my company was ordered out on the target range for practice. We had had but little practice, only being there six days when orders were received to prepare to leave our post at a moment's notice. Those were memorable days. History was being added to, or rather made, almost daily. Every one was talking of war with Spain, its results and possibilities. Our camp was in a commotion, expecting war to be declared at once. Everything was put in readiness for marching. In this condition we remained until April seventeenth, when orders came at last for the Twenty-third to proceed to New Orleans.

The city of Laredo gave our regiment a grand banquet before we left there. Every man, woman and child, apparently, who could get out to see us off, turned out.

The Twenty-third Regiment had been stationed at Laredo for eight years, and during this time great attachment had been formed between the soldiers and citizens. From Laredo to San Antonio was a long run, attended by nothing of interest. At San Antonio the citizens demonstrated their patriotism and hospitality by having a grand banquet awaiting our arrival. Every man seemed to have a good time while there. Before our train left, the citizens put several kegs of beer in every car. This was appreciated very much, as beer seems to be a soldier's favorite beverage, and one that he will have if he has money and is where it can be bought. A soldier rarely refuses beer when offered to him.

From San Antonio a run of forty hours carried us into New Orleans on April nineteenth.

For a month we were there on guard duty. The majority of the regiment seemed to enjoy their stay in New Orleans, but for me it was anything but enjoyment.

The citizens were very kind to all soldiers, and seemed to regard them very highly; when one went into the city he was generally given all the beer he wished to drink, and made to feel welcome.

Soldiers care very little for anything, and do not seem to care very much for themselves or for each other. They know that the responsibility rests upon the officers, and that food and clothing will be furnished as long as they are in the army. When a soldier draws his pay, usually the first thing he looks for is some place to gamble and get rid of his money in a few minutes, then he can be content. He is restless as long as he has a dollar, and must gamble or take some friends to a saloon and drink it up, then go away drunk.

If one man has any money and expects to keep it he must not let others know of it, for they will expect him to spend it for all. Generally when one man has any money it is free to all, and it is enjoyed as long as it lasts. Soldiers are very generous and good-natured men; if not that way at first they become so before a service of three years expires.

Army life is dangerous to the morals of many young men. They will take up some bad habits if they have not power and determination to control themselves. It is very easy for a man, especially a young man, to take up some bad habits and lead a different life altogether in a short time after he becomes a soldier. A man soon learns to drink and to gamble, although he may have known nothing of these vices before his enlistment. I thought that a soldier's life would suit me, but after a service of three years I can truthfully state that it was not what I desired. Life in camps at one place a little while, then at another place, winter and summer, rain, sleet and snow, with twenty men in one wall tent, is very disagreeable, unhealthy and unpleasant. I spent one month in camp in New Orleans during the hot weather, and all the pleasure I had there was fighting mosquitoes. We had a fierce battle with them every night.

My regiment had all the service at New Orleans they wanted in the line of guard and special duty. Four hours of hard drilling five mornings in each week, special duty in the afternoon, then half of every night fighting mosquitoes. May was very hot. I believe that the battalion and skirmish drills, without stopping to rest or to get water, were very injurious to the soldiers.

I know that they injured my feelings very much.

I was a private in Company "A," Captain Goodale in command. I thought a great deal of my captain; he was a good officer, and was soon promoted to major of the 23d Regiment, and commanded it for several months. He was then promoted to a lieutenant-colonel and assigned to duty with the Third Infantry, then in the Philippines. After he set out to join his new regiment I never saw him again. He was the first captain I served under.

Soldiers who served under good officers were fortunate, but if they had bad ones they were soon in trouble and had a hard service. A son of Lieutenant-Colonel Goodale, who was a lieutenant, was placed in command of Company "A." He, like his father, was a good officer, and soon won the confidence and esteem of his company.

After the declaration of war between the United States and Spain, the 23d Regiment was recruited to its full quota of one hundred men for each of twelve companies. Four new companies had to be formed, which were called, at first, skeleton companies, because they only had a few men transferred to them from the old ones.

Non-commissioned officers were transferred to the new companies and placed in charge of the recruits, to drill and prepare them for duty.

Drilling recruits is hard work, and all the officers avoided it as much as possible. From the 20th of April to the 24th of May we had nothing but drill.

When Admiral Dewey destroyed the Spanish fleet in Manila Bay, orders were sent to the 23d Regiment to proceed at once to San Francisco. It will be remembered that we had gone to New Orleans under orders directing our regiment to Cuba, but everything had changed so suddenly that we were ordered to San Francisco to be in readiness to go to the Philippines.

The orders from the War Department were received by

Colonel French on the night of the 23d of May.

The following day everything was put in readiness for leaving for San Francisco, but to hasten preparations all our tents were struck at 4 o'clock in the evening. Soon afterwards it commenced raining for the first time during our stay at New Orleans. Our tents were down and we had no place to shelter and pass the night. We were ready to leave next morning. I never saw so many wet soldiers before. I was on guard and saw two hundred men or more go into stables that were near our camp. We were camping in the race track of the city fair grounds, which were surrounded by a great many stables. This was rough fare, and I could not say whether the men slept or killed mosquitoes. One thing I know beyond question: I saw the toughest, sleepiest looking lot of men next morning that I had yet seen in my military service. They all seemed to have colds. To add to our discomfort all the rations had been boxed and marked for shipping, and we were without food for breakfast. Those who had any money were allowed to go out and buy something to eat. It is plain that if a man had no money he went without breakfast.

The men were all formed in line with gun, belt and knapsack, and were kept standing ready to march at the command, until one o'clock in the evening before taking up the march of three miles to the railroad station. We marched through the city and to the station without a halt. It seemed to me the hottest day I ever knew. It had been nearly twenty-four hours since I had eaten, and I think my condition was no worse than that of the whole regiment, with but very few exceptions.

We were in the city of New Orleans, and rations were plentiful, but it seemed they were scarce for us. This, however, was only the beginning of what we were to get accustomed to in a few months.

At two o'clock on the 25th day of May, our regiment boarded the cars of the Southern Pacific Railroad and set out on its journey for San Francisco. The regiment was divided into three sections for the journey, which was made in six days.

The rations issued to us on this journey consisted of hard tack, canned tomatoes, canned salmon, and last, but not least, nor more desirable, canned horse meat. To use a soldier's expression, such "grub" is almost enough to make a man sick to look at, but this made no difference, we had to eat it.

I have seen a few people who seemed to think soldiers were not human beings like other people. They thought they could endure anything and would eat any kind of stuff for rations.

While eating supper one evening in our camp at New Orleans, the men were seated in their usual manner on the open ground grouped around their mess kits containing their rations; a young lady with her escort was passing through the camp and observing the men eating supper, remarked to her companion that the soldiers looked like men.

She had possibly never seen a soldier before.

At another time a man with two small boys were looking over our camp and talking about the soldiers, when one of the little boys noticing the soldiers eating, and seeming to be interested in their manner of eating, said: "Papa, will soldiers eat hay?" His youthful curiosity appeared to be fully satisfied by the father answering: "Yes, if whiskey is put on it."

Crowds of people were out at every city and town we passed through awaiting our arrival. Some had bouquets of beautiful flowers for the soldiers containing notes of kind words and wishes, and signed by the giver. Some gave us small baskets of nicely prepared rations. These were what suited us most, and were very highly appreciated by every one who was fortunate enough to get one.

Our train passed through many places without stopping. We saw crowds of people at those places with bouquets and various gifts of kindness and appreciation which they had no opportunity to give us. Whenever our train stopped it would only be for a few minutes, and there was only time enough to receive the little tokens of kindness and good will, exchange a very few words, and we would again be off.

## Chapter III

TRAVELING THROUGH WESTERN TEXAS and the plains of New Mexico is very mountainous and lonely. Villages of prairie dogs here and there seem to be about all the living things that the traveler sees. These little animals burrow deep in the ground, thousands of them close together, and this is why it is called a prairie dog town. I was told that these little dogs live mostly on roots and drink no water. I give this as it was told me, and do not know how true it is. One thing which I noticed was that we would travel two or three hundred miles and not see any water courses.

The section that I was with was detained about three hours at El Paso, Texas, on account of some trouble on the road ahead of us. Many of us took advantage of this to look about the city. A considerable change of temperature was noted, it being much cooler than at New Orleans. Before the next morning we were passing through New Mexico. It was cold enough to wear an overcoat, but as we only had blankets every man had one drawn close around him, and was then shivering with cold. This cold weather continued until the Rocky Mountains were crossed, and we began to descend the Pacific Slope.

Crossing the deserts of Arizona was disagreeable. The white sand from a distance looks like snow, and is so dry and light that it is lifted about by the wind. Some places it will drift several feet deep. The railroad company kept men employed all the time shoveling sand from the track. Nothing but some scattering, scrubby bushes grows in the deserts. Almost any time looking from the cars there seems to be smoke away off in the distance. This is nothing but the dry sand being blown about by the wind.

Where the railroad crossed the deserts they are from one hundred and fifty to two hundred miles wide.

The first place we stopped after crossing the Rocky Mountains was in the city of Los Angeles, California. The good people of Los Angeles had a bountiful supply of oranges and other nice fruit, which were given to the soldiers, who enjoyed them very much. Some towns where we stopped the citizens would put two or three crates of oranges in every car of our train.

The country was beautiful, orange groves and orchards of different kinds were numerous and fine.

California is the most beautiful country I have seen in my travels from Georgia to the Philippine Islands.

The Oakland Ferry was reached about ten o'clock on the morning of the first day of June. Our regiment commenced to cross at once over to San Francisco. A detail was left to take our supplies from the train and load them on boats, all the balance of the regiment going across. My first sergeant was unfriendly to me and included me in the detail as a mark of disrespect to me, although it was not my time to be placed on detail duty according to the system of rotating that duty.

Our detail worked very hard for about two hours and seeing no prospect of dinner we crossed over into San Francisco to find something to eat. We found our regiment just ready to enjoy a grand banquet prepared by the Red Cross Society. It was prepared near the piers in a long stone building; long tables were piled full of all that a crowd of hungry soldiers could wish for, excellent music was furnished while we did full justice to the feast before us. The Red Cross has spent a great deal of money since the commencement of the Spanish-American war; it has accomplished much toward softening the horrors of war by caring for the sick and wounded, providing medicines and necessaries for their relief, and doing many charitable acts too numerous to be enumerated here. Many men to-day enjoying health and strength were rescued from what must have been an untimely grave had not the work of the Red Cross come to their relief when sick or wounded. The army physician frequently was a heartless, and apparently indifferent man about the ills of his patients. While at Camp Merritt I was sick for a month. The physician pronounced the malady fever; he did not seem to care about my recovery or that of any other man; his chief concern seemed to be that of obtaining his salary of one hundred and twenty-five dollars per month. Beyond this his interest seemed to cease, and if a sick soldier recovered he was considered lucky.

There were many sick men in Camp Merritt in the months of June and July. We were stationed there for five months.

Twenty-five men, myself included, volunteered to be transferred from Company "A" to Company "E." This transfer was made on the sixth of June, and was done to fill up Company "E" to its full quota for the purpose of going to Manila on the transport *Colon*, which was to leave San Francisco on the fifteenth of June.

My company, now Company "E," was being prepared by Captain Pratt, and was drilling for the last time in the United States before going to Manila. I unfortunately became ill and had to be left at Camp Merritt to go over later. It was sad news to me, for I wanted to go over with this expedition.

One battalion of the 23d Regiment was left at Camp Merritt, which included my old company, to which I was assigned. We stayed at Camp Merritt until about the middle of August, when orders were received to go to Manila. By the time everything was packed and ready to strike tents a second order was received, not to go to Manila, but to go to Presidio, in San Francisco, and await further orders. About the 10th of October, to our great joy, orders were read out at parade in the evening, that we would start to Manila on the seventeenth. The men were so glad they threw up their hats and shouted for joy. We were glad to leave the cold, foggy and disagreeable climate of San Francisco, and delighted that we were going to Manila, which was then the central battle field.

The bad climate, incidentally mentioned, of San Francisco seemed to be only local, extending along the coast for only a few miles.

I have been in San Francisco when it was cold enough to wear an overcoat, and going across the bay to Oakland it was warm enough for a man to be comfortable in his shirt sleeves. The distance between these two points is only six miles. The native citizens of San Francisco, and those who have been residents for many years and accustomed to the damp, foggy atmosphere, are very healthy.

But this climate was very detrimental to the soldiers in Camp Merritt, and fatal to many.

While stationed in Camp Merritt I spent a great deal of time in the San Francisco park, which contained one thousand acres of land.

A great variety of wild animals and many different kinds of birds were there, and I found in it a great deal of interest and amusement. Crowds of people were there every night. Many people were there for the purpose of committing some crime. People were frequently being sandbagged and robbed, or sometimes boldly held up, and money and valuables secured.

I knew a great many soldiers who were robbed, sometimes they received bruised heads just by loafing in the park at night.

No reflection is intended to be cast upon the police whose duty was in the park; there were a great many of them, but they did not know all that was being done in the park, and it was necessary for a man to keep a sharp lookout for himself if he wished to escape uninjured.

The date of our departure the Red Cross gave a fine dinner for all who were going to leave the camp. This was the custom with that society when any soldiers left there for the Philippines.

All those who left while I was there partook of a splendid dinner just before leaving.

This society, in addition to the dinner given to us, had several hundred dollars worth of provisions put on board our transport, and all marked, "For enlisted men only on deck."

At three o'clock in the afternoon of the seventeenth day of October, 1898, we sailed on board the transport *Senator*. The provisions put on board for us were well cared for—by the officers, who took charge of them and guarded them so well that if an enlisted man got any of them, he had to steal them from under a guard. Actually had to steal what belonged to him by gift, and if caught stealing them he was court martialed, and fined enough to buy his rations for a month, but the fine money was not appropriated in that way.

We had a rough voyage, not on account of the weather, but because the transport was so packed and crowded that a man did well to walk from one end of the ship to the other. We were crowded like a cargo of animals bound for a slaughter pen.

A private may think all or anything he pleases, but he does not have an opportunity to say very much about anything. He must obey the commands of his officers.

Our officers on the transport had everything to suit themselves, and the private had to do the best he could and try to be satisfied, or at least appear that way.

It would take two-thirds of the deck for half a dozen officers to have room. They thought themselves so superior to the privates they did not want to be near them. Our ship had fifteen hundred men on board.

We reached the port of Honolulu, after several days' sailing on rough seas, October twenty-fifth; five days were taken to coal for our long voyage to Manila. Honolulu is a fine city, about 2,190 miles from San Francisco. Located as it is, away out in the Pacific Ocean, makes it the more attractive to a Georgia soldier who was on his first sea voyage. There are some fine views in and around Honolulu. As our transport steamed into the harbor of the city I

## A Soldier in the Philippines

thought it a grand sight. From what I could learn I had but one objection to it as a desirable place to live—leprosy is too prevalent. A small island is used for the lepers' home, where all who are afflicted with this most loathsome of diseases are carried, yet the fact that those poor victims are in that country is a disagreeable one and makes one shudder to look at the island. No one is allowed to go there, except on business, and they have to get passes from the authorities to do so. I had no desire to visit the place.

Honolulu is a very good city, with some of the modern city improvements, such as water works, electric lights, street railroads and ice factories. These are the results of emigration, people of other countries going in with money and experience. The natives are called Kanakis. Agriculture consists in the cultivation of rice, bananas, cocoanuts and coffee. It was there where I first saw bananas, cocoanuts and coffee growing. A lieutenant, with about twenty-five men, including myself, went out about six miles along the beach. We went to the Diamond Head, six miles eastward from Honolulu. This is an old crater of an extinct volcano. Returning to the beach we went in bathing and enjoyed it very much.

Our party had to get passes and present them to guards on going out and returning. Our transport having coaled and made all the necessary preparations for the voyage to Manila, we went on board and sailed about four o'clock in the afternoon of October the thirtieth. But few of the soldiers had been sea-sick before arriving at Honolulu, but after leaving there many of them were ill for several days.

I think that the native drink called swipes was the cause of much of it. This had been very freely imbibed by the soldiers. It is a peculiar beverage, producing a drunkenness that lasted several days. Some of the men getting over a drunk on this stuff, by taking a drink of water would again be drunk. I escaped sea-sickness and, but for the fact that we were living on the transport like pigs in a crowded pen, I would have gone over comfortably and would have enjoyed the voyage.

Our rations were very poor, scarcely fit for hogs to eat. They consisted of a stewed stuff of beef scraps, called by the men "slum;" prunes, hard tack and colored hot water for coffee. Once a week we had a change from this of salmon or cod fish. I believe those who shared this food stuff with me on this voyage will bear me out in the statement that it was tough fare.

The soldiers were not alone on board—there were other passengers who seemed to dispute our possession and waged war on us both day and night. These belligerents were known as "gray backs," some of them being nearly one-fourth of an inch long and very troublesome. Clothing and everything else seemed to be full of them.

I have seen soldiers pick them off of their bodies and clothing and kill them before the men went to bed, hoping to get rid of them and get to sleep.

I have seen several times almost the whole body of soldiers on board sick and vomiting. There was something peculiar about this sickness. Nevertheless, it was true; the men were fed on rotten prunes and fruit, which, after nearly all the supply was consumed, was found by our surgeon to be full of worms. This had been the cause of so much sickness. By refusing to eat this rotten stuff myself I was not ill.

About half way between Honolulu and Manila an active volcano was passed about four o'clock in the morning. Everybody went out on deck to see this great sight. Although it was raining at the time the men stood out in it to see this remarkable spectacle. It had the appearance of a round hill sticking out of the water, the whole top burning and falling in.

## Chapter IV

THE MOST INTERESTING SIGHT I ever beheld was in the China Sea. One evening, just before dark, when the sea was rough and black, threatening clouds were hovering over us, lightning shooting its fiery bolts across their path, and every indication pointed to one of those fearful typhoons for which the China Sea is noted. The crew had closed all the port holes and hatchways preparatory for the storm, which was believed to be fast approaching. While yet on deck with a number of soldiers, who were looking across the surface of the rough waters, there suddenly appeared in the water an object that looked like a woman; it had long hair just like a woman; the upper part of its body was like a woman, and to all appearances was a woman. It rose about half out of the water and sank back. Three times it did this and disappeared. I learned that this strange sea animal was a mermaid, and that they are seen during such stormy weather as we were then experiencing.

Another very interesting sea animal is the porpoise. It is shaped something like a fish, except the head, which looks like that of a hog. They will follow a ship in droves, swimming near the surface of the water and jumping out of the water and diving down like fish playing.

I have seen many living things in water, some of which were very interesting looking that I never heard any name for. A very strange, helpless-looking object is the star fish. They are often left by the tide on the beach and are perfectly helpless until another tide carries them back. A flying fish fell on deck of the transport and was picked up, greatly exciting our curiosity. This strange little animal never gets more than a few inches long. These fish go in schools; sometimes a school is so large that it covers half an acre or more, skipping or flying along on the surface of the water sometimes one hundred yards before striking the water again. I had in my hands the one that fell on our deck and examined it with a great deal of curiosity. It had a pair of small wings and was very beautiful.

The jelly fish does not look very clean and nice. The largest one I ever saw was eighteen inches thick and looked like a mass of jelly and was hard in the center. These fish are of two colors, white and black. They can sting when they touch the naked body and give as much pain as the sting of a yellow jacket.

I have been in the water bathing and one of them would sting me, making a great, red, burning spot. I have seen sea serpents, but was never close to one where I could see it plainly. They seem to be very easily frightened, and I only saw them on the surface of the water at some distance. They are very large snakes with black spots.

The men on our transport were interested in a flock of sea gulls, which to us appeared to be the same birds following our vessel to pick up the scraps thrown overboard. I could see them any day and I therefore believed they were the same sea gulls. They can fly farther than any other bird.

We arrived in Manila Bay November twenty-second, and anchored about two miles out from the piers of the city. The view was delightful to all on board, especially the soldiers. We were happy and jokes were freely passed around. We were once more to be on land and what person would not be happy over this thought after so long a voyage over the great waters of the Pacific?

Five days we had to wait before quarters could be obtained and we could land. I was very anxious to get away from that transport, which to me was worse than a jail. I never was jailed in my life, but I believe that two months' imprisonment would have been more pleasant than the time I was on board that ship. Finally we were landed at a point just below the Bridge of Spain and marched into the walled city of Manila. It will be remembered that a portion of the Twenty-third Regiment had preceded us a few months. Our landing would reunite the regiment, and to celebrate the occasion that portion of it that went over first had a banquet dinner prepared for our arrival. It was a memorable occasion long to be cherished by my division of the regiment. After such disgusting food as we had had since leaving San Francisco we appreciated the elegant feast and plenty of Manila wine that was set before us. This latter portion of the regiment did full justice to the occasion, both provisions and wine, which was excellent. We stayed in the city and performed guard duty for a few months. It was of the hardest sort all the time that we were in the Philippines. It was performed day and night part of the time.

We had "running guard," which was day and night, but this would not continue more than a week at one time. Manila was then a dangerous place for Americans and our guard and patrol duty was desperate work.

All the citizens of Manila were our enemies as long as the Spanish soldiers remained in the city; when they were sent back to Spain conditions improved immediately.

No one was permitted to go out of the city. The citizens were allowed, at intervals of several days, to pass out through the sally ports of the wall and take two hours' exercise in the Lunetta, which is the favorite outing grounds of Manila, and a place for executing insurgents. This was a privilege not often granted, and when the people were thus indulged they had to be back on time.

Aguinaldo, with his army, was just outside of Manila from the time the Americans captured it until his attempt to enter and capture the city from the Americans. This attempt was made on the night of February ninth, the first demonstration indicating his intentions being made about nine o'clock in the night. The Filipinos attempted to enter through the sally ports and were promptly discovered by the guards, who commanded a halt. The command was not obeyed and the guards fired upon them. This seemed to be the signal for a general engagement by the Filipinos. The Nebraska Volunteers were the first to receive the attack of the enemy. At once the battle became furious and continued for several days and nights. The enemy was making a desperate and determined effort to enter the city, but failed, and were finally driven back to a position where they could be easier handled by our forces. After about ten days' fighting the Americans threw up works and entrenched themselves and waited for re-enforcements before taking the offensive. The American forces numbered ten thousand in the city and the enemy's forces were estimated at sixty thousand. The American lines were getting too long and weak to risk an attack and we held our position and waited for re-enforcements to arrive. During this time the Filipino prisoners were closely guarded and forced to bury their dead. Five days were occupied in this work of picking up and burying the dead Filipinos. The number of their dead is unknown, but must have been large. It was reported that five hundred Filipinos were buried in one day. It was also reported that eighty Americans were killed in one night.

I shall never forget that night attack; I was one of three men on guard in the Spanish hospital. This was a very dangerous post at any time, but on an occasion like that it was more so. Three hundred Filipinos were in the hospital, about one hundred prisoners and about sixty Spanish women. All the hospital corps of attendants were armed with some kind of weapon, usually a knife. When the attack was made on the guards at the wall and the firing commenced, I was sitting in a chair and almost asleep from exhaustion and continued guard duty. A Spanish woman in the top story of the hospital heard the firing. She ran down to where I was sitting, took me by the shoulders and was shaking me vigorously when I first realized what was taking place. She was very much excited and jabbered at me in Spanish, which I had no knowledge of and did not understand one word she said. When she saw that she could not make me understand her Spanish she went away. I heard the firing and knew that an attack was being made. The Filipinos in that hospital would have met with little resistance from only three guards had they made a dash for liberty. They could have easily passed out through the unlocked doors while we could have killed a few. After gaining the outside they could have given assistance to their comrades, and in the darkness of the night set fire to the city and made our situation a desperate one indeed. The Filipinos knew the city much better than the Americans and had Aguinaldo been possessed with the nerve and ability he could have entered with his superior numbers and captured the city. The Filipinos, however, gave the Americans some hard fighting before the enemy's forces were scattered over the island of Luzon. After the Filipinos were scattered they divided into small bands, which marched over the island burning and destroying. One of the bands when run upon by the Americans would give them a short desperate fight and flee to the hills in safety. Frequently it happened that a squad of American soldiers would be outnumbered by a band of the enemy, and it was then the Americans turned to run into Manila for safety.

A great many of the native business men, both employers and employees, stayed in Manila after it was captured and carried on their business. Many of these were a menace to the safety and the authority of the Americans. All the arms and ammunition and dynamite that could be obtained by them were hidden away. They banded together to do all the mischief possible, but our guards were too clever for the Filipinos and always detected their schemes and plots before they could be carried out. It was believed that the men inside of the city were working with the enemy outside for an outbreak. Aguinaldo would engage the attention of the Americans and these treacherous Filipinos and Spaniards inside would do a great deal of mischief before being discovered.

Therefore, in the face of all this, much depended on the efficiency of our guard duty. Guards were on duty in all parts of the city, in church towers and every place that would give any advantage in keeping a lookout for any indications of trouble.

## Chapter V

BEFORE AGUINALDO'S ATTEMPT to enter Manila the friendly natives outside the city were suffering from a fatal epidemic of some character, apparently so, judging by the number of caskets taken outside. This continued for several days; one or two caskets every day were allowed to pass out by the guards, although orders were issued to search all boxes, trunks and baggage; yet these caskets were allowed to pass through unmolested for about fifteen days. Finally the guard's suspicion was aroused by these frequent burials and it was decided to open a casket, which was packed full of Mauser rifles. This ended the funerals outside. This demonstrates the trickery and smuggling schemes of these people.

I have known prisoners to escape by exchanging clothing with their wives, who were permitted to visit their husbands in jail, the man passing out and leaving the woman in prison. A great many prisoners escaped in this way before the scheme was discovered.

Dummy guns and soldiers were placed in forts in a manner to deceive Americans as to the strength of the works, but the Americans were not to be bluffed so easily and this scheme was worthless.

Almost the whole American force was on the streets of Manila watching and expecting an attack for two weeks before it was made. We were always prepared to fight. We had to keep our clothes on all the time and our guns and belts by our side. I did not have more than fifteen nights' rest from the 20th of January to the 24th of May. Frequently we would just get on our bunk when a call to arms would be given; every man would rush out in a hurry and sometimes had to march four or five miles, before stopping, through rain and wind, or whatever weather we might be called out in. There we would stay the balance of the night. If we wanted to lie down we only had one blanket to put on the wet ground. Every man had to look out for himself and get the best place he could.

We would only be in a few hours from one march until orders would be received to march to some other dangerous point; it appeared that we were only marched back to the city to take a bath and change clothing, which we needed.

I believe these marches in the night or day, in the hot

## A Soldier in the Philippines

climate of that country, lying on the wet ground sometimes every night for two weeks, has killed more men than were ever killed by the Filipinos. Those who never died from the exposure died from the kind of rations they ate out on the lines. It has been a mystery to me how I ever reached America again. I have been through everything and have seen as hard service as any soldier in the Philippines, and have eaten as hard grub as any of them ever ate.

I believe the Twenty-third had call to arms no less than twenty-five times. Every time we thought a fight was on hand and we would see some fun with the Filipinos. Whenever we got them started to running, which most always was easily done, then the fun was on. We were sent out a great many times to guard some town from the enemy's torch.

Company "E," of the Twenty-third, was detailed to guard the first reserve hospital in Manila and was on duty ten days. The officers feared that enough of the enemy would slip through the lines to enter the hospital and commit many depredations and kill the wounded Americans, so we were detailed to guard it and walk the streets and hold up every vehicle of the Filipinos and search them for arms and ammunition. This holding up and searching gave the sentries all they wanted to do. All the time we were there on duty we could not leave without permission. We laid about in the hot sun in the day time and at night on the ground. Some of the soldiers pulled grass and made beds to sleep on the side of the streets.

The only thing to help pass the time while on this duty was to go through the hospital and look at the wounded, some with arms off, others with a leg gone, while there were men wounded in almost every imaginable way to be living. Some would get well when it looked almost impossible for them to recover. I have seen thirty to forty wounded piled in a box car and sent into Manila, where they were put on a boat and carried up the Pasig river to the hospital. They were taken from the boat and put in a cold place till the doctor puts them on the operating table and handles them like a butcher handling a beef. Almost every day women and children were brought in with burned hands and feet, the Filipinos burning every town which they thought was about to be captured, and the women and children suffered; doubtless, many were burned to death.

Fire is a dangerous resort of the Filipino. About one hundred got through the lines into Manila and made an effort to burn the city, but the promptness of the Americans saved it, only five blocks being burned. The soldiers were kept busy guarding the negroes and keeping them away from the buildings. Big stores were burning and the fire department was too poor to save them; the proprietors told the soldiers to go in and get anything they wanted.

While the fire department was doing all it could to save the city and sneaking Filipinos were hindering the department all they could by cutting the hose. They would assemble in crowds and then the hose was cut; every one caught in this act was shot down on the spot. Six or seven were thus punished that night. It was an exciting time and looked as if Manila would be burned in spite of all our efforts to save her. The Twenty-third Regiment did guard duty all night on the west side of the city. The enemy, failing to burn Manila, fired a little bamboo village outside; the bursting bamboos could be easily heard by us. The noise was just like that of guns and the Filipinos took advantage of this noise to shoot at us in the city. They would get behind the light of the burning village and when an American could be seen in the light of the burning houses in Manila he was shot at. This was kept up all night. Our great trouble was to distinguish between the noise of the bursting bamboos and the report of a Mauser rifle. The noise of bursting bamboos could be heard three and four miles, some of them not much unlike a six-inch gun, and the reports from a burning bamboo village was almost a reproduction of a battle and would last several hours.

After guarding the burning district of the city all night

## A Soldier in the Philippines

we returned to guard duty at the hospital. Orders were received to march to the firing line at San Pedro Macati. We marched there on the first day of March and stayed till the tenth. We were in trenches at the front; our provisions were more than half a mile at the rear and details were made out each day to bring up provisions to the men in the works. These details were fired at in going and coming by the Filipinos, but their fire was ineffective, owing to their distance from us, until the detail neared the trenches, where the distance was not so great, and it was very dangerous. Some were wounded.

A man behind the works could not get out for a few minutes' exercise without being fired at, and if he did not get under cover soon they would get him. I have seen many men shot that way; they thought the Filipinos could not shoot. I have seen some fine marksmen among them. They could do some good shooting until they became excited and fled for some place of safety.

I have seen squads of Filipinos come near our trenches and open fire on us. A squad of Americans with their arms would jump out of the trenches and start towards them and they would soon disappear like so many frightened deer. I was in a squad of soldiers who ran three Filipinos for two miles. They were shot at several times, but got away.

We were out ten days and had two engagements; we had a very hard time on this excursion. Water was hauled two miles and a half on a two-wheeled vehicle, in old vessels holding four or five gallons. By the time we could get to the kitchens about half of it would be spilled.

Buffaloes were used like oxen in this country. They were much larger, however, of a dark brown color and very easily frightened. When one started to run away no man could hold it. I have seen them run as fast as a good horse. Their horns were of immense size and flat, considerably extended. They generally did not turn aside for smaller objects when running away. On one occasion I saw one run against a stone building, knocking himself down. He arose and ran on as fast as before. Those that run at large will get in the water where it will cover them and stand with their noses out for half a day.

The fourth day out at San Pedro Macati we had a bush skirmish and some hard fighting for about two hours.

This was my first fighting and I have to confess to being a little frightened this time, but kept my nerve on all other occasions. We ran them back from the trenches and out of sight. They were not to be seen even by the aid of field glasses any more that day. We could not estimate the number of killed, as they left none on the field.

The first sergeant of my company was slightly wounded in the chest by a spent ball, from which he recovered in a few days. I was near him and heard the bullet strike him; it almost felled him. This was the first soldier I saw wounded.

The way the bullets were coming I thought every one of us would be killed, but no one was shot except the one just mentioned. Out-posts were always stationed two hundred yards or more from camp every night, or in front of our trenches, to prevent a night attack. If the enemy started through our picket lines they were fired on by the pickets, who would then rapidly fall back to our lines of trenches. This out-post duty is very important and very dangerous, especially when the sneaking Filipinos were in the community.

Many nights the Americans would be aroused from their slumbers by the enemy's attacks and efforts to surprise them, and we would lie in our trenches and fire on them till they left. The enemy would be stationed on an opposite hill and they would sometimes get very close to our out-posts, who could see them moving about and talking and hear them walking in the leaves and underbrush. Our sentinels had orders not to fire on them unless they made an attack, when the sentinels fired and got back into the trenches as quickly as possible to escape being killed by our own men.

They violated the custom of the white flag frequently. A party of six or eight would leave their lines with a white flag

## A Soldier in the Philippines

and advance a little and wave the flag. A party of Americans would start to meet them.

Every time the Americans stopped the Filipinos stopped. They tried to get our men as near them as possible and when they thought they could get our men no nearer they would seize their rifles, which they would have concealed behind them, and fire on our soldiers. Their scheme evidently was to kill all the officers they could, but they only succeeded in killing two, as far as came to my knowledge. After a few attempts of this kind they were fired on regardless of their white flag scheme.

While at San Pedro Macati the First Colorado Volunteers would go out and sleep all night on the hill-top. Some one was killed, or wounded, every night this was done. But few Americans were killed before the advance was made on the enemy. A strong post was taken and many Filipinos killed and captured. Ninety were captured in one little bamboo village of a dozen houses. This was the morning of March tenth. That evening orders were received to return to Manila. We had been in the trenches the greater part of the ten days at San Pedro Macati, and had two engagements, one the fourth and one the tenth of March.

We set out on the return to Manila late in the evening of March tenth. We had a march of six miles to make. A heavy rain drenched the soldiers, reaching the walled city of Manila about eleven o'clock that night.

After a few days' rest Company "E" of the Twenty-third went up the Pasig river on cascos to Laguna de Bay, a distance of fifty miles from Manila. This is a body of fresh water twenty miles wide and sixty miles long, and deep enough to float a large steamer.

A gun boat, which stayed there in the bay, and of the same name, was boarded by a part of our soldiers and steamed up the bay for the purpose of capturing Santa Cruz. We had to go up in front of the town in full view of the Filipinos, who saw the approach of the gun boat and left in haste for the mountains.

Our boat grounded and we had to wade out a distance of two hundred yards. The bottom of the lake was uneven and by the time land was reached we were wet from running into holes of deep water. On reaching land a line of skirmishers was formed and the town was entered without any trouble. But one Filipino was seen. He was almost frightened to death. With the aid of field glasses we could see Filipinos on the mountains. When we left they returned, but before going we burned some large buildings in which supplies were stored, mostly rice and sugar. We returned to the gunboat and cascos late that evening.

Captain Grant, of the gunboat, wanted to go about thirty miles up the bay from Santa Cruz. We made the run in three hours. It was a very bright moonlight night. The objective point was reached about eight o'clock. On getting very close to shore an old priest was seen on the dock waving a big white flag, which he continued to wave until we landed. Captain Pratt took an interpreter with him and learned from the old man that everything there was all right. He informed Captain Pratt that he thought the town would be bombarded if not surrendered without it. There was a fine church at this place; the town was built of bamboo. A few stores and about four hundred Filipinos were there. The Filipinos had gone to the mountains while we were landing, but returned when the old priest rang the church bell as a signal that all was well. We were preparing to sleep in their bamboo houses, but Captain Pratt, fearing some treachery, ordered us to the cascos and gunboat to sleep, but as we were wet and muddy large camp fires were built where we could dry and eat our salmon and hard tack before going on the boats.

We had had some hard service for four days and felt very much like sleeping, but the boats rolled and plunged until we could not sleep. We were in a dangerous place. Had all the Filipinos who came into that place that night been around they could have given us a hard fight, and possibly have killed us, but, fortunately, they did not appear to have any arms. Next morning two cascos were loaded with captured wood and we left this place to go down and across the lake to take another town.

Our boats were anchored two miles out and an armed detail sent out in a small launch to reconnoitre. It was found to be too strong for our forces. A strong fort and almost three thousand Filipinos were in the town. We remained in front of this place until the next morning watching for Aguinaldo's gunboats. He had four in the bay. One had been captured. Just before dark one of these gunboats was sighted coming around the point of an island. It was going into port, but seeing our boats it turned back. We made no effort to pursue this vessel, as our boat was slow of speed and night was coming on. Nothing more was seen during the night and next morning we went down the lake to the Pasig river, which is the lake's outlet. Going down the river about five miles we awaited orders from Manila.

We were out on this expedition for ten days, part of this time on the Laguna de Bay and the remainder in the Pasig river.

We had a good time after starting back towards Manila, but little to do and less to care for. While awaiting orders on the river we consumed a great deal of time hunting chickens and ducks. These were very plentiful and easily caught. We fared well on these every day for a week. We also killed all the hogs that were necessary to supply our wants, and there were plenty of them. The first ones were killed by Lieutenant Franklin, who took a rifle out one evening and was gone almost an hour. At last he returned with two fat pigs which he had shot. We expected to enjoy eating them the next morning as they had to be dressed and cooked. Next morning our hopes and expectations of a good meal were exploded by finding that the pigs were spoiled. After that we profited by that experience and always ate our hogs as soon as they could be prepared. The trouble about keeping fresh meat there was the hot, moist climate. This would soon spoil it, especially if not dressed immediately after being killed.

On the ninth day of this expedition about twenty-five

men went out on a hunt for porkers. Six very good-sized ones were secured by this party, to which I belonged. Another expedition went duck hunting and bagged eighty fine ones. Great numbers of chickens were everywhere in the woods and towns. They belonged to the natives. A party of soldiers caught fifteen of these while the hogs and ducks were being secured. These three parties returned about the same time loaded with the spoils of the chase.

The cooks tried to please every one and set us at dressing our game. They cooked every hog, chicken and duck for dinner that day. There were about ninety men in this company. This was one of the last three days out on this expedition of ten days. The other seven were very rough and hard ones for us.

One night some of the men made a new arrangement about sleeping. The day had been hot and clear and the open air was desirable to sleep in where we could enjoy the full benefit of a nice cool breeze which was blowing. The deck of the gunboat we thought an ideal place to spend the night. We were very sleepy. This spot was free from mosquitoes and we were preparing for a fine rest. Captain Grant looked out on deck at our positions and said: "Boys, look out up there tonight. It rains here in this country sometimes." The sky was almost cloudless and we thought nothing of rain.

About two o'clock I awoke, thoroughly drenched, and the rain falling as fast as I ever saw it in my life. Any one who has not seen it rain in a hot country has an inadequate idea how hard a tropical rain really is. My blanket was perfectly wet and the water was standing on one side of me in a pool. It took me so by surprise that I was bewildered. Finally I decided to leave that place and seek shelter. I wrung the water out of my blanket and groped about in the inky darkness and went into the engine room, where I stayed until morning. That drenching rain seemed to affect all who were exposed to it and resulted in severe colds in every instance. The twenty-fourth of March we were about fifteen miles from Manila, up the Pasig river, awaiting orders. The Pasig river is deep and wide, large steamers being able to traverse its waters. A strong under current made swimming difficult and dangerous.

Observing some soldiers across the river at a deserted bamboo village I decided to go over to them. I set out and swam till tired. Looking back I discovered that I was about half way across the river. I swam until I was almost too exhausted to raise one hand above the other. I could not tell whether I was moving or not, except, perhaps, down stream.

I was in a critical condition, but did not give up nor get excited. Had I done so I believe that I would have drowned. I know of about twenty soldiers who were drowned while trying to swim across the Pasig river.

By struggling with all my strength I succeeded in getting across. I did not know how I could get back without swimming and I decided not to try that. I was very exhausted and rested and planned a long time. Finally I found a piece of plank and getting on that I went across all right. This experience was sufficient for me, and after that I never went into water too deep to wade.

We left our river post and went into Manila. On the way down the river we met with an accident that might have been fatal to about fifty men. A casco had been captured in the Laguna de Bay, and about fifty men, including myself, went on board the captured vessel and were being towed into Manila by a launch. Our vessels had to pass under the Bridge of Spain. The captured boat was too high and in attempting to pass under the bridge the whole top of the casco was torn off, timbers and fragments of the broken vessel were flying in every direction, and it looked as if the men could not escape these missiles. I was in the stern and thought that half of the men on deck would be knocked out into the water and possibly drowned. Quicker than it takes to tell it, I was lying on my back in a close, narrow place where there was just enough room for me to wedge into. The casco was being pulled to pieces against the bridge and as it went farther under the bridge the rudder beam was pushed around over me with such force that it left grooves in a piece of timber not more than an inch above my face. It was that piece of timber that saved me from being crushed to death.

After the excitement had subsided a little I found that I had been struck on one side and hurt, but only slightly. The launch tore loose from the casco and before it could again be fastened another accident threatened us. Several large sailing vessels lay at anchor along the river and the casco was about to run into them. This accident was avoided and we were landed and marched into the walled city of Manila.

## Chapter VI

OUR COMPANY ARRIVED at Manila on the night of March 24, 1899. The next night our regiment was ordered out to reenforce the volunteers in capturing Malabon. This town was full of Filipinos, who were fighting the volunteer forces then trying to capture the town. Our forces marched to the north of the town and camped. Every soldier had to cook his own provisions, if he ate any that were cooked. The march from Manila to our camp was twelve miles. Every man carried one hundred rounds of cartridges, knapsack and his provisions. The site of our camp was on the bank of the Malabon river, which was reached at sunset. We had to cross the river before camping and the only chance was to wade or swim. Some could wade, but those who were short had to swim. We wanted to cross without getting our blankets and provisions wet, but some were more unfortunate and lost them. I tied my blanket and provisions to the bayonet fixed on my rifle and crossed with them dry, but my person suffered by the water and mud. Night had come on by the time the regiment reached the camping side of the river and guards had to be put on duty at once. Our blankets were piled up for no further service while we were out on this expedition; the men, wet and muddy, had to pass the night the best they could. There were supposed to be from 3,000 to 4,000 Filipinos near by and our night camp was a hazardous one. Everything must be done with the utmost caution.

The men, wet and muddy, fought mosquitoes all night and had no rest. The Filipinos could be heard all night busily tearing up the railroad track and destroying a bridge a few hundred yards from us. They dug pits in the ground and built fires in them, over which the track rails were placed till hot enough to easily bend. Bending the rails, they thought, prevented the Americans from using them again in shipping supplies over the road. The site of our camp was a low, mucky place on the river bank, where mosquitoes literally filled the air.

That was the hardest night on me of all the nights of two years' service in the Philippine Islands. I was so sleepy and tired next morning that I could scarcely hold up my head, and my condition seemed to be no worse than that of every other soldier in the regiment. Mosquitoes had bitten me through my trousers and brought blood. Frequently I have been sleeping after a hard day's service when the mosquitoes would bite my face and the blood run out and dry up in hard drops. When I could not get water to wash off these places I would scratch them off. In some cases these bites were poisonous. I have seen soldiers with large sores, caused by scratching mosquito bites. I was cautious about poisoning during my service in the Philippines.

The morning of the 26th, about four o'clock, I saw from my post, where I had been all night, a big fire in the direction of Malabon. The Filipinos had fired the town and left it. It was our purpose to capture the place and take some forts on the river, but the tricky Filipinos preferred burning their town to surrendering it to the hated Americans.

Our forces took up the advance on the enemy, who stubbornly resisted us from ten o'clock in the morning until four in the evening, when they retired to Malinto and took another stand behind a stone wall and held this position until driven from it by a charge. We had to advance up a long slope of open ground for one and a half miles. Firing was kept up rapidly all the way. The enemy was driven out and the town taken. About thirty men were killed and wounded on the American side. The enemy's loss was not known, but must have been very heavy.

One poor fellow who was among the wounded in this battle I remember very distinctly. He was first sergeant of Company G, Twenty-second Regiment. He was shot through the head. The doctor dressing the wounds as he came to the wounded saw this sergeant and said there was no use to do anything for him, that he would die in a few minutes. The wounded man replied that he would live longer than the doctor would and wanted his wounds dressed. He lay there and talked to his comrades, who were around him, and cursed the doctor for neglecting him. He remained in this condition an hour or two and died.

After a short rest in Malinto we marched about one mile south and back to Malinto again. That night we marched to a point near a station on the Manita and Dagupan Railroad and camped. We were then about eight miles from Manila, and opposite Malabon, which is off the railroad and on the beach near the mouth of the Malabon river. Our camp was located more than two miles from where we had left our blankets that morning on going into battle. A detail of ten men, including myself, was made out to go after the blankets. They were obtained and we returned to camp with them about ten o'clock that night. We had to cook our rations for supper after our return, but being rather a frugal meal of easy preparation but little time was required to prepare it; frying some bacon in mess kits composed all the cooking; hard tack and canned tomatoes composed the remainder of the meal. The ground with the starry heavens

## A Soldier in the Philippines

overhead and one blanket was both house and bed. The next day we marched into Manila, arriving about twelve o'clock. We remained there doing guard duty till the 30th day of March.

In the evening of the 29th orders were read out to provide three days' rations, fill our canteens and each man to be furnished with one hundred and fifty cartridges. We all expected a battle and were anxious for it, but did not know where we were most likely to get it. Every one was busy and anxious to be marching, especially the officers, who usually could hardly wait for the time to come after receiving orders to march.

We were to have supper on this occasion at five o'clock, but all we had were some scraps and crumbs from the camp kitchen.

Our orders were to march to Maricana, which was held by the enemy. We marched twelve miles before camping. It rained before we started out from Manila and cleared up, but left the roads very muddy and made marching very hard. The twelve miles were made by ten o'clock. That night the wet ground served as couch and one blanket as all the covering. We had to recline, if we lay down at all, with gun and belt at our side, ready at a moment's notice to meet the enemy's attack should they swoop down upon us in camp. After a halt of six hours we set about at four o'clock preparing breakfast, every man cooking his own rations in camp kit and making coffee in a quart cup.

Men were gathered around their little fires of wet wood on the damp ground trying to burn wet wood and cook over the little fire it made. Some of the hungry men had just succeeded in getting their fires to burn and commenced to cook when orders were given to prepare for the march to Maricana, which we were expected to capture that day and to take the Filipinos prisoners or drive them into the neighboring mountains. It is needless to say that those men who failed to get their breakfast were ready to fight. They had an opportunity before many hours passed.

From the camp it was five miles to Maricana. The march began at four-thirty, while it was still dark, and we could move unseen by any of the enemy who chanced to be lurking in our vicinity. We marched through the woods and without speaking above a whisper marched close to the enemy before we were discovered. Their sentinels in the church towers were the first to discover our approach and give the alarm by ringing the bells.

Maricana is located on the bank of a river and we advanced within one hundred and fifty yards of the opposite bank before we were discovered. We advanced at double time and reached the river bank, when we lay down and opened fire just as the early daylight was appearing. Our skirmish line covered the whole town, in which the enemy were stationed as a reserve force to their advanced lines along the river. This advance, or outer line of the enemy, were fortified behind a stone wall. Our line was at the disadvantage of being in the open ground. The lines thus formed were hotly engaged for some time when the command was given to cross the river and charge the enemy's lines. The river bank in front of me was about ten feet high, but this offered no obstacle to me when bullets were falling thick and fast near by. At the command to cross I jumped and somehow got down the bank and into the water. Looking back I saw no one else coming. The bullets were coming around me so fast I had no time to form any plans and I pushed on into the water until it was almost over my head. I remained in this condition until I saw my command crossing about one hundred yards below me. I could not get out on the bank to go down and decided I would wade down to the crossing place and join our forces there. I was almost exhausted when I reached the shore. The enemy, seeing our intentions to attack their line, remained behind the stone wall and fired at us until we were nearly across. Then they could stay there no longer and fled from their strong position. We crossed and entered the town, capturing five armed men. The enemy beat a hasty retreat,

## A Soldier in the Philippines

rather a pell-mell flight across the open country towards the mountains, at whose bay they had entrenchments and a large reserve force. The fight lasted from daylight till about two o'clock in the evening. The battle of Maricana was as hard as any fought in the Philippine Islands. About three thousand American soldiers were engaged. Several were killed and a great many of the Filipinos.

When an American was wounded his wound was dressed and some soldier's blue shirt hung up near him to designate the place where a wounded American was. In this way no one would be left on the field after the battle when the dead and wounded were picked up.

The Filipinos were not so well cared for. I saw a great many soldiers run out of their way in order to step on a dead or wounded Filipino. They would shout with joy at their punishment of the poor Filipino.

I was near three Americans who were shot that day; two of them were killed. The one who recovered was a member of my company. A ball passed through his body, entering the back and passing out on the right side. It didn't seem possible for him to live, but in one month he was again at his post of duty. A lieutenant of the Fourth Infantry had his horse killed under him. Jumping off he took out his field glasses and got on his knees and began looking for sharpshooters. In less than a minute he was shot through the heart and fell dead without speaking. I thought every second I would get a bullet, for they were flying so thick and close that I did not see how I could escape them. Before the battle was over I wished I might be shot, for I never was so nearly dead in all my life. My condition did not appear to be any worse than that of every other American soldier.

We were run almost to exhaustion and were awfully hot. I drank water that day from ditches and holes when the water looked green and tasted very badly. I knew the water was filthy and even dangerous to drink, but I was not going to die for water when there was plenty of it near by. During the heat of the battle I was lying down near an old soldier.

We were both trying to get cover. We were fighting hard with no protection but the ridges in a large rice field which we were fighting over. Our firing line was in a line of skirmishers. A bullet hit the ground in front and between the old soldier and where I lay. It knocked dirt in our faces. The old soldier looked at me and appeared to be very much frightened. I only laughed at his funny looks. Before I got away from that position I felt a hard shock on my chest. I thought that I was shot at last and put my hand up to examine the wound. Finding myself all right I looked at the ridge and saw what it all meant. A bullet was buried in the ridge. I dug it out with my bayonet and kept it, and I have it yet as a souvenir of that day's battle. I have several more bullets which struck near me at different times and places. All of these I treasure, for I do not expect to get any more bullets just as I did these.

The American loss at Maricana was twenty-four killed and nineteen wounded.

## Chapter VII

AFTER LEAVING THE BATTLEFIELD we returned to the camp we had left that morning. The whole force was almost exhausted by the day's service and marching was a slow, burdensome task. A great many men lost their provisions in the battle or in crossing the river. Mine was lost in the river together with my mess kit, canteen and haversack. Those who were fortunate enough not to lose their rations of canned beef and hard tack were enjoying a hasty meal. At this juncture orders from Manila were to march to Caloocan Church that night, a distance of about twenty-three miles. It was then getting late in the evening and this march to be made before camping was not very pleasant news to already

## A Soldier in the Philippines

footsore and tired soldiers. Before marching out of sight of our camp men began falling out. I marched about half an hour and had to fall out of ranks and straggle along as best I could. My company set out for Caloocan with one hundred and twenty-eight men, only eighteen of whom marched through that night. The others were scattered along the route, footsore and worn out. Many of them pulled off their shoes to relieve their blistered feet and marched barefooted and carried their shoes in their hands, and, like myself, stopping almost every hundred yards to rest a few minutes. We were afraid to stop long at a time. We would have become too sore and stiff to move.

We continued to move along in this tedious, toilsome way as rapidly as possible. My party of three were proceeding as best we could. In the darkness of the night we lost our way by taking the wrong road and went into a small town, where we found a few white men, one of them a doctor belonging to the First Regiment of Colorado Volunteers. He made many inquiries about us and our regiment and asked all about the battle fought that day. He looked after our welfare by providing us with shelter and beds, but there was something else we wanted before sleeping. We were perishing for food and all we had between us was a small can of bacon, a ten cent United States coin and one small Spanish coin (a paseado). With these we went out to buy bread. We found a Chinaman and bought a piece of bread that was so hard we could scarcely eat it, but we made a very good meal on that and the bacon.

We slept on a good spring bed and I awoke next morning in the position I was in when I fell asleep. I was so stiff and sore that it was miserable to have to move. After breakfast we went into Manila and took the railroad for our command.

A number of soldiers arrived after we did and reported for duty. All the provisions that I ate on this expedition, which lasted three days, would not have made more than one good meal. Before my party reported at Caloocan one of the other two and myself were reported captured by the Filipinos, or lost. That night we all went back into Manila to resume guard and patrol duty. Police duty was all done by soldiers until a force of Macabees was organized. The Macabees are enemies of the Filipinos, and soon became our allies and were very good soldiers and police.

Manila has a population of nearly 400,000 people of different tribes and nationalities. It is the capital of Luzon and the most important city of the Philippine Islands. The energy and enterprise is due to foreigners. There are several miles of narrow gauge street railroad and a system of electric lights.

To mingle with these people it is necessary to know two or three languages, if not more. Spanish is the prevailing language. Most of the business men can speak several languages.

The Chinese are the filthiest people there. I have seen hundreds of them living in their workhouses where a stench was arising too great for a white man to approach. These filthy people cook, eat and sleep all in this filthy hole. Their principal food is rice and soup. One dollar of United States currency will buy enough for one person to live on a whole month. When the Americans first entered Manila it was very filthy. The air reeked from the accumulation of filth during the siege of the city. This made the place a little worse than usual. It took the soldiers three months to clean out and clear out the streets.

The only thing apparently that kept down a great deal of disease and death is the continual blowing of the sea breeze.

Those killed in battle outside the city had been carried in and buried in shallow holes, or probably I would be more correct in saying, about half covered with earth and left that way for dogs to scratch up and pull about by the arms and legs.

I have seen dead Filipinos carried out of the hospital, thrown on carts and carried to the burying ground and handled like dead hogs. They would be covered a little and left to the dogs. I don't believe I ever looked towards the place without seeing dogs there eating and pulling the bodies about.

## A Soldier in the Philippines

Hundreds of beggars are to be seen squatted down at all public places and on the street corners. They do not sit down like Americans. This is the case with all the natives. They sit in a peculiar, squatting way, which is positively tiring to any one else but these natives.

The Filipino men wear trousers rolled up high and a long white shirt of very thin material, the tail hanging out over the trousers like a sweater. They wear nothing on the feet and most of them wear nothing on the head. They are not fond of clothing, and many wear very little, almost going nude. They find a great deal of pleasure in the possession of a gun and it seems that they are content with a gun, fighting and running in the mountains. They care little for life and will fight till killed.

A squad of Filipinos was captured near Manila by some of the Fourteenth Infantry; when they were approached to give over their guns to the soldiers they would make a motion like giving up a gun, but instead jump back and attempt to shoot a soldier. If he succeeded in shooting an American some other American would shoot the Filipino. Several were killed in this manner.

When a Filipino is captured his greatest desire is to keep possession of his gun, and sometimes fight for its possession after being captured.

The Filipinos are a natural race of gamblers; they gamble and trade, many of them, for a living, refusing to work as long as they can get anything to eat without working for it. Their principal cause for idleness is the cheapness of their living, rice and fish being their principal food. They will catch fish and throw them in the hot sun for two or three days; they are then taken up and smoked and burned a few minutes over some coals and chunks, and then eaten.

If any Americans are watching them they will say, "mucho chico wino," while eating this delicacy of their indolence and filth. The Filipinos and native tribes are extremely filthy in their eating, as well as everything else; they eat almost anything that an American will refuse to eat.

The Macabees is another negro tribe on the Island of

Luzon. They are a much better people than the Filipinos and more intelligent. This tribe is hostile to the Filipinos, and fight them whenever an opportunity is offered.

Two regiments of the Macabees were organized and equipped by the Americans, and placed in the field against the Filipinos, and they made very good soldiers.

## Chapter VIII

I MISSED BEING PLACED on a detail of twenty-five men to serve on a gunboat; I wished to get out on some kind of service and leave the regular and dull service in Manila. I missed this detail in all probability by being out in the town when the detail was being made out. I tried to get on when I returned, but failed, the detail having been made out already. This detail from my company saw much more service than those remaining in the company.

Their discharges show a record of more than a dozen engagements. They served in this detail five months, and had plenty of hard service. They were only paid once during the five months; a few of them, however, were not paid until discharged, if I was correctly informed. Their descriptive list was lost, causing two men to have to serve ten days longer than they enlisted to serve.

Much "kicking" was done by men in other parts of the service who were not paid for a year or more, but all to no purpose.

I was on the alert for another detail to be made and to get on. At last I succeeded, on the tenth day of April, in getting on a detail of only ten men to perform guard duty on a dredge boat that was dredging at the mouth of the Malabon river. This was twenty miles from Manila. The object of the dredging was to make a channel in the shallow water at the river's mouth sufficient to enable gun boats to enter the river, which was deeper after leaving its mouth. This was very slow work, requiring a great deal of time and labor to perform it. This dreging had been going on for a month. We were on duty there for ten days, and, judging by what I saw, it must have required two months' more work to open the desired channel.

From our station numbers of natives could be seen on shore, and passing up and down the river. It seemed that the country was full of Filipinos.

We watched them a great deal. Their methods of catching fish was very interesting to us. They never used a pole, hook and line as we would. At night great crowds could be seen, each one in a boat, and carrying a big torch. They would be near the beach, going out but a little way from the edge of the water; they would beat and splash in the water, and drive the fish into large traps or nets, just like a hunter driving quail into a net, only the fishermen were more noisy.

After beating the water and banks until it was supposed the fish had gone into the net, or trap, they were left in it until next day, when they were seined out. Great quantities were caught in this way.

Another method of fishing was to get in a boat with a long gig and move the boat slowly, and when a fish was near enough gig it. The large fine fish were only caught in this way.

Our detail returned to Manila in the evening of April tenth, and remained there until that portion of the 23d Regiment was ordered to the Island of Jolo, where we started on the seventeenth day of May. I had been in the old walled city of Manila a little more than six months; part of my regiment had been there ten months. We had had very hard service there, and the close confinement, almost like imprisonment, made us glad to change, and held out a hope that we would find easier service and more interesting.

The wall of the old city of Manila extended entirely

around the old city. The sally ports and all the streets were always guarded until no soldier could go outside without exhibiting a pass to the guards signed by the company and commanding officers. All the time that I was stationed there I was never out without the required pass.

Guards were stationed on top of the wall, and made it unsafe to try to climb it to get out, although I have seen this done by means of a rope; men would pass out this way and stay out as late as they wished to and return.

This was not safe. Even the guards did not discover the attempt, for the wall was not less than thirty feet high, some places even higher, and forty feet wide. Stone houses are built in this wall, and used for military stores. On top of the wall on the sea-side were three hundred large cannon when the city was surrendered to the Americans. Around the old Spanish arsenal about two acres were covered with cannon balls, guns, bayonets and rifles, all scattered about in a mass until it was difficult to get over the ground. It required two months of the American's time to pile up and arrange these munitions of war surrendered by the Spanish.

After the treaty of peace all these were returned to Spain.

A great many Spaniards live in Manila, and are subjects of Spain. They have some very peculiar customs. One that came to my notice is that of the courtship of a Spanish youth and his sweetheart.

The young man is not permitted to enter his sweetheart's home, but stands on the outside and makes love to her though the iron bars of a window. I saw a great deal of this before I learned what it all meant.

The Spanish seemed to have a very bitter hatred for all Americans just after the fall of Manila. When we first entered the city the Spanish women would throw anything that menaced us in passing the streets, from their windows. They would do anything to harass and endanger the lives of Americans that they could think of without exposing themselves too much. Starvation was staring them in the

## A Soldier in the Philippines

face when the city was surrendered. They had been reduced to rice almost wholly for sustenance. The pay of the Spanish soldiers was very small. I was informed that it was only six dollars Spanish per month, equivalent to only three dollars of United States currency. Yet this meagre sum had not been paid for several months.

A Spaniard is not a very frank, attractive looking fellow to an American soldier. He has a sneaking countenance, and a disposition out of harmony with that of the American. However, this opinion may be modified somewhat with those able to speak Spanish and become better acquainted with them. Being unable to speak their language I was barred from this possibility.

Luzon and some other large islands are very fertile, and under proper agricultural management would yield millions and blossom as the rose, but as yet they are blighted by the uncivilized natives. A man would be taking his life in his hands to go out into the country and try to engage in anything. As conditions existed when I was there, bands of hostile Filipinos were scouring the whole interior, and frequently were bold enough to raid near the American posts, leaving devastation wherever they went. The soil is very fertile, a warm temperature and plenty of water to irrigate with if desired for that purpose.

The natives use the most crude implements, and have but very little knowledge of farming, and are too indolent to put into practice what little they do know of soils and crops. It seems to make little difference what season they plant in. The climate is always warm, most of the year extremely hot; too hot for an American or white man, to labor in. It is just the climate that suits the negro. Chinese and negroes work for fifty and sixty cents per day.

A very fine tobacco is raised, and most of it exported. A cigar factory in Manila manufactures a great quantity of cigars.

Rice is easily raised, and is the principal food of the natives.

The rough rice is husked in a very crude way; a wooden trough, or dug out, is used to put the rough rice in, and chunks of wood are taken in the hands, and the rice is pounded with these until the husks are all broken off, the rice taken out and separated from the husks.

Sugar is an important crop, and is extensively raised. No less than fifteen sugar mills could be counted from the top of the walls of the city of Manila.

Under improved methods of agriculture that country would be a wonderful one in the production of sugar and rice.

The Philippines will, in all probability, become important in the near future in the production of minerals, principally gold. There are some very good veins of gold ore in the mountains of Luzon, some of which I saw myself. Several pieces of stone on which gold was easily seen, were picked up by the men of my regiment. I saw rocks with both gold and silver in them. The men would not tell just where they had found them. They probably thought that at some time, after their service expired, they would return and work the places found.

I knew one man, an old, experienced miner, who would spend the Sundays out in the hills and around the foot of them, where he was not exposed too much to the enemy, prospecting for gold. He was successful in finding good indications of rich minerals. He appeared to make a confidant of me. At one time he showed me a lot of gold and some silver that he had found out on his prospecting tours, but would not tell me where they came from. He told me that when he was discharged he intended to return and work the mines. I knew that the paymaster had considerable money belonging to this old miner, who told me he should invest it in the mines, and in purchasing mining machinery.

I saw and heard enough to cause me to believe that when the natives are civilized, and when men would be safe in the mountains, that the mines in the Philippines will attract more people than the Klondike ever did. There are

## A Soldier in the Philippines

advantages in the Philippines which are not found in the Klondike region, the most important being the climate, not considering the quality of the mines, which I believe to be equal to that of the Klondike.

The mountain regions are rich in various minerals.

In the Island of Mindanao coal has been mined ever since Americans have been there.

This country will find out in a few years what is in the Philippines. I believe it is a rich country. Almost anything can be raised that is desired in the line of field and garden crops; fine timber is plentiful and saw mills are yet unknown. I don't believe there is a saw mill in the Island of Luzon. All sawed timber is imported that is used at present; not much is used in building as most of the houses are built of stone or bamboo. The frame buildings which we have in America are never seen there. All the native houses and small towns are built of bamboo, and covered with grass. The bamboo grows very large, the joints are two and three feet long, and some of the larger bamboos are as large as a common tree. They are the same thing that people in this country know as canes, the difference being in their size only. Houses are built of bamboo without the use of nails. Nothing for flooring but the naked earth. Split bamboo is worked into the houses fastening the whole together. I have seen the natives build houses, and have no other tool than a large knife. The roof of grass is fastened on with strips of bamboo, and is three to four inches thick. This roof is superior, in point of comfort, in a hot country, to that of anything I ever saw. I have been in the hot sun and in metal roofed buildings, and on going into a grass covered house the difference was noticeable immediately, the grass roofed house being much cooler.

Manila is built of stone; the buildings look very old, but are good yet.

One night when the Thirteenth Minnesota Regiment was on police duty, and no one was allowed on the streets after seven o'clock at night, with a fellow soldier I started out to go to a dance outside of the city walls; we knew that if we were caught we would be court martialed. To avoid all the risk possible we went out before seven o'clock, and took chances on getting back to quarters safely. We could not return to our quarters without passing sentinels, that much was certain, but how to pass them safely was the question then most important to us. I had an army pistol, and with that in my hand I directed my friend to play the part of a prisoner and march before me. We proceeded in that way only a short distance when a guard halted us. I explained that I had a prisoner carrying him to headquarters. The guards were to see orders for a pass or whatever orders I might have, but this one allowed me to pass on with my prisoner without showing any orders. We passed in by all the guards and patrols on the streets, and were halted and some questions asked and answered, but none of them asked to see any orders regarding my prisoner, who all the time was just in front of me. I was afraid that every guard and patrol would demand my orders, and then our scheme would fail, and we would be in trouble. I told them it was late and I must hurry in with my prisoner, and so we passed them all and reached our quarters in safety. The men worked a great many schemes to get out and in, but it was for my friend and myself to play the part of prisoner and guard first.

I never tried any more schemes on the guards, but was always in at night; I did not like to risk so much just for a little fun. We were very careful about keeping our little scheme from the officers, but told some of our comrades about it, and enjoyed the joke with them.

## Chapter IX

ON THE SEVENTEENTH day of May the Thirteenth Regiment and two battalions of the 23d Regiment went on board the Spanish transport, *Leon*, and sailed for the Island of Jolo.

I was a member of one of the battalions of the 23d. We boarded the "Leon" under a Spanish crew and sailed under the Spanish flag. The "Leon" was a large vessel of rapid speed, and made the run from Manila to the Island of Jolo in a little more than forty-eight hours, a distance of 800 miles south of Manila. Land was in sight almost the entire voyage. We passed through straits and seas, by Iloilo on the Island of Panay, Cebu, Negros Island, through the sea of Jolo to Zamboanga on the Island of Mindanao, and to Jolo. The group of islands forming the Sulu Archipelago is the southern islands of the Philippines. The "Leon" sailed into the Jolo Bay in the evening on the nineteenth of May. A large force of Spanish soldiers was stationed in the town performing garrison duty. Our force was to relieve them, and they were to return to Spain on the transport *Leon*. On the twentieth of May we went ashore. The Spanish soldiers seemed to be very glad to be relieved and return to Spain.

The garrison was short of rations, and the soldiers were living very hard when we relieved them. These Spanish soldiers were the last who left the Philippines for Spain.

We were landed in small boats, which could not carry very many men. The boats were rowed by Chinese. All supplies have to be carried in by these small boats. It is a very slow and tedious piece of work to land the contents of a large ship, and requires several days to do the work.

Captain Pratt was in command, and Company E was ordered out to the block house, which stands about one thousand yards back of Jolo, and towards the mountains. A guard detail was made out, and the Spanish soldiers were relieved. I relieved the first Spanish of his post at Jolo. When I approached him he began to speak in Spanish and tried to make me understand what, I supposed, were his orders he was turning over to me. I could not understand him, and told him to go. Of course I had enough orders without his, if that was what he was trying to explain to me.

The Spanish went to work with a rush getting everything

ready to leave. They had been there for a long time. I learned that the commanding officer, who was an old man, had been there twenty-eight years. In the evening at two o'clock the Spanish flag on the block house was hauled down by the Spanish soldiers and the Americans unfurled to the breeze the Stars and Stripes. The Spanish seemed to be very much grieved, the officers wept; the Americans were jubilant. Everything passed into our hands, and the various responsibilities of the place with all its dangers also passed to us. The natives, who belong to the Morro tribe, are treacherous. We knew nothing about them and their intentions. Guards were put on duty at once, six being around the block house so that a Morro could not get in if the attempt were made to enter it, and thus made it a place of security to our troops. The Morros a few years ago massacred more than one hundred Spanish soldiers in the block house Astora. It was a cruel and treacherous piece of cunning of savage barbarians. The Morros had been warring against the authority of Spain, and causing the Spanish troops much trouble. At last apparently tired of rebelling, the Morros agreed to make peace with the Spanish. According to an ancient custom of the Morros, when making peace with an enemy they would give pearls or some other gift to their enemy. The captain of that Morro company was going to make peace, according to this custom, and taking some fine pearls and a body guard of one hundred of his men he entered the enclosure where the Spanish soldiers were lined up in two columns with unloaded arms to receive them. The Morro captain and his body guard marched between these lines, and as the guard neared the Spanish captain the Morro advanced with his pearls, and getting near the Spaniard instead of giving him the pearls he quickly drew his sword and dealt the Spanish captain a death blow. The Morros, who understood the prearranged treachery, opened fire on the Spaniards, who were helpless with unloaded guns, and the entire garrison of more than one hundred men was massacred except one man, who, in the noise and consternation, succeeded in crawling into a sewer pipe, and through it into a big stream of water, and escaped without injury. The Morros gave the Spanish a great deal of trouble, probably as much as any other tribe of the Philippines. The Morros have a bad record. I believe that I had rather fight the other tribes than the Morros; they are more treacherous than other tribes. They go armed all the time with the bolo, a large knife carried in a wooden scabbard. From the oldest man down to little boys, they all carry the bolo or a big knife. I have seen old men, so feeble they could scarcely walk, carrying a fine bolo. They will not part with them day or night, but keep them as their only friend, refusing to let any one take them from their hands to merely look at them. These arms are very fine, and range in cost from five to fifty dollars. They are manufactured of the very finest steel, the handle of many of them is made of silver and finely engraved. The edge is kept very sharp. The blow of this dangerous weapon is generally enough to kill a man. I was informed that a Morro never struck his enemy but two blows with his bolo, one on each side; if that did not disable him the Morro would run for his life.

A steel armor is worn by a few of them, to furnish protection to their bodies. But most of the tribe would rather risk their life than wear anything, even clothing. Only a piece of cloth is worn around the waist and loins. In this piece of cloth is carried a box containing a stuff to chew called beadle nut. Only the married men are allowed to use this, as they have a law prohibiting its use by the single men. It is a soft green nut growing on a tree which looks very much like a hickory tree. A piece of the nut is placed on a leaf, which is always carried in the chewing box, and some salve is also placed on the leaf, then the piece of nut and the salve is rolled up in the leaf, and the chew is ready for use. The married men can be very easily distinguished from the unmarried ones simply by the use of this, which makes the chewer's mouth as red as red paint and the teeth black. The teeth of the single men are very white, but just as soon as one marries he begins chewing beadle nuts, making his mouth red and teeth black in a few days. Their marriage customs are not exactly like ours in America. A Morro can marry a woman, or buy one for a price ranging from fifty dollars up to one hundred and twenty-five dollars. After marrying a woman or buying one, if she doesn't suit her husband he doesn't have to wait for a court to set aside the marriage, but can simply let her go and proceed to get another in the same manner.

The men are prohibited from having a plurality of wives at one time, but are allowed to have just as many as they desire, simply getting rid of one and then getting another.

The women wear big legged trousers, which only reach down to the knees. Sometimes women are seen with more clothes on, but they look as if they were torn almost off. The clothing of both men and women is worn out before they ever change. A few who lived in the towns wore more clothing than those in the country. The men wore pants which seemed to cling to the skin, they were so tight. Those in town were no cleaner than outsiders. They get so filthy and slick that an American can smell one as far almost as he can see. The more clothes a Morro wears the filthier he is. Those wearing no clothing, except the girdle around the loins, are the less filthy. Nothing is worn on the head and feet.

Leprosy is a common malady, as well as numerous other diseases of the skin. All of which doubtless arises from the filthy habits of the people. Doby itch is very common. It is a very bad skin disease, and hard to cure when it gets a firm hold, and will have fatal results in a few years in that warm climate. One doctor said that it would require three or four years' careful treatment to cure an acute case of doby itch in another climate.

Almost every day I saw a bad case of it. The legs will become swollen, and large knots and tumors cover them until walking is extremely painful. It is easy to contract doby itch. About two weeks after I reached Manila the first time, I

## A Soldier in the Philippines

discovered a small sore spot on my leg, which looked like ringworm. I was informed that it was doby itch, and that I should have it doctored before it spread. I began to treat it, and it itched seemingly to the bone, and began to scatter. I would wake at night scratching and clawing the itching spot, and lie awake for two and three hours. I had to trim my finger nails closely to keep from ruining my leg scratching it. It continued this way for several days before I checked it. Many of our soldiers had a similar experience, some of them much worse than mine. I guarded against it afterward, using all the precaution I could to avoid it. A friend of mine who enlisted when I did, caught a severe case of the doby itch which kept him in an almost helpless condition for eight months. He was finally discharged for disability, a wreck for life, without anything but a small pension of about eight dollars per month.

To the Morros again. There is a class whose religious teaching is that when one of them kills seven white men he will go to a better country when he dies. He thus makes sure of his entrance to what is heaven in their religious belief.

The Americans soon learned to distinguish one of this class, and watched them very closely. One of them will not wait for much of a chance to kill a white man, but will make his chance to do his deadly work. I have seen a great many of them, and know that they attempted to kill our men on duty as out-posts. They would not have any guns and would go to the walls of the fort and try to scale them to get to the Americans and kill them with bolos. Without trying to kill them the soldiers would shoot towards them to drive them away. When one of their number dies the grave is dug one day and early the following morning the funeral begins. Every one carries something to eat, a big bottle full of beno (a native beverage) and a bottle of whiskey. Four men carry the corpse on two small poles, all the others fall in behind in column of twos and then they proceed to the graveyard, drinking their beverage and enjoying themselves. The crowd stays at the graveyard all day, and drink and carouse until they are well filled with liquor, and all get drunk. This is the program every time one of them is buried. It is a big picnic for them.

Once a year regularly they prepare some of the best rations they have and carry them to the graves and leave them there through the night, believing that these are enjoyed by the dead. I learned that this was an ancient custom of theirs, having been learned probably from the Chinese.

The Morros seem not to care for anything, not even for life. A large number, probably two-thirds, never had any home. They did not know where they would go, and seemed not to care.

Some of the islands had two or more tribes of negroes, who would have a governor to each tribe and make laws for themselves. If natives of one tribe crossed the line into the territory of another and stole fruits, cocoanuts, of anything else, and the injured tribe could catch the thief or thieves, their heads were cut off and their bodies left on the spot. This is according to their laws. Beheading for theft, and leaving the bodies where they were beheaded. I have seen five or six in this condition two or three times.

One tribe would sometimes array itself against another for battle and fight till great numbers of them were killed. Our troops stopped several such battles by going out where they commenced to fight. As soon as we would arrive they would stop fighting, and there seemed to be an end of the trouble between them. They appeared to be in great fear of our guns. They have a few old rusty guns, which are only used to fight enemies of other countries; never using them to fight each other with. When General Bates made a treaty of peace with the Sultan of Jolo, the sultan was received by General Bates the first Sunday in May, 1900; we were drawn up in line and presented arms to his excellency. The sultan was to maintain peace on the island of Jolo, for which he was to receive 500 dollars Mexican coin every month. We presented arms to him, and were forced to treat him with

# A Soldier in the Philippines

great honors. I can assure the reader that for myself it would have been more pleasant to have gone out to meet him on the battlefield, and when I speak thus I feel safe to make the assertion that many more were of the same disposition.

After these formalities were over I had opportunity of examining the guns of the sultan's body guard, also the ammunition. The guns were so rusty that I would have considered it safer to be shot at by one of them than to shoot the gun. The barrels were almost closed with rust.

A lot of the bullets were wrapped with cloth, and stuck in the shells. Some of the bullets were loose, and some were driven in very tight. All of the shells had the appearance of being in use a long time, and that they had been fired as many times as they would stand.

A man was taking his life in his hands to go out into the country alone. Many people have been killed in this way. There is a tribe that would cut off a man's head for amusement, or to see how it looks.

Guards were kept on duty all the time, and no American was permitted to go outside of the wall without having a pass. This was kept up for a long time after we went to Jolo, and was then restricted to one thousand yards from the fort, and no less than four men together. The Morros gave us very little trouble, doubtless the result of extreme caution. They never had an opportunity of making any demonstration, so it is uncertain what they would have attempted had the opportunity been given them. They are too treacherous to be trusted about anything whatever.

They have very little knowledge of firearms; probably the only guns they ever had, and also those of the sultan's body guard, were old, worn-out guns given or sold to them by the Spanish. With our improved rifles I believe that one man could withstand the attack of twenty of them armed with bolos, that is to say, were the American in some fortification, and opened fire on the Morros when they came in his range. They, of course, would not fight in this way, their method being one of sneaking treachery. They slip up behind the unsuspecting victim and behead him with their bolo.

I was anxious for them to engage the Americans in a fight. I desired to know something more of their methods, but they seemed not to care to fight us. They are a wandering people, seemingly with no definite purpose. As night suits their sneaking better than open day time they do as much traveling, or more, in the night than in the day time. They could be seen on the hills around Jolo with torches moving about all night. When we first went to Jolo and saw these torches at night we thought they were signals, and close watch was kept on their movements.

They evidently made some preparations for resisting us at first, and stored away such arms as they could obtain, for later I saw twenty-eight new Mauser rifles hidden in an abandoned house on the beach. Another soldier and I secured a pass and went, at the risk of our lives, beyond the limit of our pass, and on this outing discovered the hidden Mausers. We went up the beach about fifteen miles, and went into two towns where there were a great many Morros. We watched their movements very closely, and kept at some distance from them, and never bothered anything or any one. They watched us very closely, and acted to us very strangely, but made no effort to get near us. We were a little frightened and thought it safer to get away from them, when we started on our return, the nearest and quickest route that we could. Our pistols were no doubt the instrument of keeping them away from us, and at the same time tempted them to kill us to secure them.

Some of the soldiers were afterwards killed, and their guns and cartridges taken. It was very dangerous for two or three men to be out in the woods away from any help. In the mountains of Jolo and Mindanao are wild cannibals, who would kill and eat a white man should he be found in their midst. We were not allowed to go out in the mountains, but the places where we were prohibited from going by orders of the commanders were the places most desirable of all for us to slip out and go to. The dangers to us by going out were only fascinating rather than hindering.

It was my belief while there that the natives were gathering up and storing away arms and ammunition preparatory for resisting the Americans when they thought the proper opportunity was offered. The guns I saw hidden in the house on the beach, and many other things, led me to this belief. They claimed to have some big guns posted back in the mountain. Whether this was true or not I am unable to say, for we never went to ascertain the correctness of the story. While stationed at Jolo a vessel arrived loaded with ammunition for the sultan. It was discovered and taken into custody by the custom house guards.

## Chapter X

ALL THE LARGER ISLANDS have an abundance of game, wild hogs, chickens and deer. Wild dogs are plentiful in the woods. They are very wild, running off almost at sight of a man. At night they seem to be bolder and come around the outside wall and howl so much that people are kept awake all night.

A detail was sent out by our commander's orders to lie in hiding and shoot them when they approached near enough. We could see them away off during the day in the grass, but could not get to shoot them. The only chance for that was to hide at night and wait for them. We frequently went out and killed a number of nice fat wild hogs and carried them in and feasted while they lasted. These animals were very wild, like the dogs. A man on the ground could not get near enough for a good shot—they would discover him and run. We would climb a tree and wait for them.

The town of Siasse, on Tai Tai Island, was the station of Company H for three months. Morros almost swarmed on the island. The captain of the company permitted a squad of men every few days to go hog hunting when the supply of meat began to get short. Some of the Morros were trusted by the soldiers and were allowed frequently to go out with the soldiers on a hog hunt, as these trusted ones were thought to be harmless. One day the captain sent out five men early in the morning to hunt hogs. They hunted until tired in the evening, when four of them sat down to rest and play a few games of cards, while the fifth went to the beach near by and bathed his feet.

A crowd of Morros, twenty or more, gathered around the players to see the game. The soldiers were not afraid of them doing any mischief, as the Morros appeared friendly and quiet. As the game progressed and became more interesting the players became less conscious of their position, and those standing around.

To be more comfortable and have better use of their bodies and limbs their belts were taken off and laid by them with their guns. The Morros gathered around the soldiers saw the opportunity for mischief and seized upon it at once. They seized the soldiers' guns and belts, while six of them drew their bolos and began their deadly work. The first soldier who was struck with a bolo had his head cut off at one blow. The soldiers were making a desperate fight for life against what seemed no chance for success. Two soldiers were killed in the fight, another grabbed for his gun; getting hold of it he received a heavy blow on the head with a club, was cut dangerously in the neck, but succeeded in securing his gun so that he could fire it. The firing frightened the Morros, who commenced running. The soldier on the beach ran back where he left his comrades when he heard the shooting, but the Morros were then out of sight. Two soldiers lay on the ground dead, another was cut so much that he bled to death before they could get him back to camp, while the one who did the shooting had a terrible wound in his neck and had received a heavy blow on the head.

It was a long way to camp, and one boat with room enough for two oarsmen. Night was almost on, and the situation was perilous in the extreme. The man who was not in the fight carried the dead and wounded men to the little boat, and set out for camp as rapidly as possible. As above stated one more died while being carried to camp, making three dead and another with his head almost half off. The sea was a little rough, and only one man rowing, with a feeble help of the wounded man with one hand, made slow progress.

Camp was reached at three o'clock next morning. The wounded man recovered but could not turn his head; when he looked around he had to turn his whole body, and was discharged from the service for disability. He draws a pension of thirty-six dollars per month. Next day after the Morros killed and wounded the hunting party, sixty men were sent out to capture the murderers. The chief of the Morros was offered a large reward for capturing them and turning them over to the Americans. The Morro chief captured them, turned them over to the Americans, who then failed to pay the reward as previously promised. Six Morros were all that were guilty; these were bound together, carried out of camp and shot.

## Chapter XI

SEASSA IS SITUATED ninety miles south of Jolo. Few of the men liked to be on duty there. At first entrance of our troops they had to go into camp, as there were no barracks. Barracks were built later at Seassa and Buangior by the soldiers stationed at these places. The captains of those companies were mean and cruel to their men, and worked them very hard. Some men were almost killed by the hard work at these barracks and in the swamps cutting timbers for their construction. Some while at work in the swamps had mud slashed in their eyes and almost put out. The mud poisoned them. Some had their feet poisoned by the black mud. The captains made the soldiers do the work, instead of hiring natives, and kept the money appropriated for this work and used it for their own benefit.

A soldier had no opportunity to report such frauds. If he wrote to the department commander to report anything without the permission of his immediate commander he would be court martialed. And of course an officer guilty of such conduct was not generous enough to permit a private to report his conduct to a superior officer, and thus the privates were ill treated by some unscrupulous officers.

The hardships of the service were greatly increased or diminished according to the honesty and unrightness of the officers in command. A private is only a tool in the hands of his officers, and can be managed just as they please as long as the private remains in the service. I always thought it better to obey all orders, agreeable or disagreeable, and serve out my time of enlistment and get a good discharge, and then be free and independent. I enlisted merely to get the experience of army life, and to know just what the service really is. I found out to my satisfaction all about the army that I cared to know. The army is all right when its officers are all right. But many of them fall far short of the standard—officers who will not give a private justice as he should.

A few soldiers deserted the army. I cannot blame a man much for it. Some had good cause. But to desert the army in the Philippines and attempt to get away from the islands is almost impossible. Any one leaving there must have a passport to present when they attempt to go on board any vessel, and then if the passports are not properly executed they cannot go on board.

I know of a few soldiers trying to get away, but the farthest point they reached was Hong Kong. They would be caught very easily.

## A Soldier in the Philippines

The one who reached Hong Kong was apprehended by English officers and returned to Manila and delivered to the American authorities.

One man who enlisted in Manila was discovered to be a spy for the Filipinos, securing all the information possible for the advantage of the Filipinos, and conveying it to them at every opportunity. This spy had gone with a company to which he was assigned, to Bungio for duty. While at Bungio he induced two other soldiers to desert their company and go with him to the Filipinos, promising each a commission in the Filipino army. He was an officer in the Filipino army, and a very dangerous man, resorting to all kinds of schemes and treachery to accomplish his purposes. Having pursuaded two soldiers to go with him they seized a small Morro boat, and with their rifles and a good supply of ammunition they set out in the darkness of the night headed for the island of Mindanao. Ninety miles of water lay before them and their small boat. They encountered a rough sea, lost their bearings, and finally the boat capsized, and they lost their clothing and one gun after a battle with the sea for three days. Instead of reaching Mindanao they drifted on the Island of Jolo, about twenty miles from the town of Jolo, almost starved to death. In preparing for their trip they had not thought as much about rations as about ammunition. They fell into the hands of the Morros, who carried them to Jolo and delivered them to the Americans, who placed them in prison. Two of the poor fellows' feet were blistered all over by marching over the hot sands, having lost their shoes when the boat capsized. These two were unable to walk for some time. They were tried and sentenced to terms of imprisonment from five to six years. This was the common fate of all who tried to desert the army and get away.

I was on duty on several islands and in many towns in the Philippines, but Jolo suited me better for service as a soldier than any other place I was in. I was on duty in Jolo for thirteen months, and know a great deal about the place. Most all the soldiers who did service there liked it. Sailors enjoyed their visits to Jolo. Quite a number of sailors told me that they had been in a great many towns of the tropical countries, but that they would rather live in Jolo than any of them. The most undesirable feature of the town is that there are no pleasure retreats except to go to the mountains and among the Morros, and besides, we soldiers were confined very closely within the walls and on duty. The town is very small. A man can walk all through in less than an hour.

I have known of recruits on going into Jolo express their delight at the idea of doing duty in such a fine place, and wish they could stay there the three years of service for which they had enlisted. But in less than two months, seeing the same things every day, they wanted to get away, and would have given anything for an opportunity to go to another post. Everything became monotonous, and seemed somehow to be wrong.

This seemed to be the common experience of all. The town is beautifully laid out with broad streets, which are set with beautiful shade trees that are green winter and summer. A person can walk all over town the hottest days and be in the shade all the time.

Three small, but very nice parks with beautiful and delightfully fragrant flowers and shrubbery lend a charm to the town.

I have been walking out in the town at night, and would smell the sweet odors from the parks for two or three blocks away. This was not occasionally so, but all the time. The soldiers enjoyed sitting in the parks and on the piers at night, taking in the cool sea breeze after a hot day. I have seen as many as three and four hundred soldiers sitting out on the piers before going into quarters.

As in all other parts of the Philippines, chicken fighting is a favorite sport in Jolo. Outside of the city wall is built a grand stand and pit for chicken fighting. It is all enclosed, and ten cents (Mexican) admission is charged unless you have a chicken to enter. Some fine chickens are entered in these fights, and a great deal of money is put up on them.

# A Soldier in the Philippines

Gambling is not prohibited, and chicken fighting is engaged in every Saturday all day long. The natives will gamble away the last cent they possess before they will stop. A suburban town of Jolo is Buss Buss, nearly half as large as Jolo, and built out over the water on bamboo poles driven into the mud, and left projecting above the water. The houses are then built on these poles.

Buss Buss is built over shallow water, running out over the water for one hundred and fifty yards. The houses are all built of bamboo. This seems to be a Chinese town. Many Chinese live there and engage in business in Jolo. Chinese are engaged in various kinds of business in Jolo, but all live in Buss Buss. The Chinese and Morros are not friendly, and it is probably due to this fact alone that caused Buss Buss to be built.

Major Sweet was in command of the post at Jolo for some time. He would not allow more than one hundred Morros inside the city walls at one time for fear of trouble with them. The Morros supplied our forces with vegetables, fish and fruit, which they brought in and sold to us. To prevent the town from filling up with Morros a strong guard was stationed at the gate, which was closed at six in the evening and opened at six o'clock in the morning. The Morros would be crowded around the outside of the gate every morning waiting for it to be opened to go in and dispose of their produce. Frequently there would be twice as many as were allowed inside at one time. When the gate was opened they would rush for it, but not more than one hundred were allowed to pass inside. When one disposed of his produce, etc., and returned to the gate he was allowed to pass out, and another from the outside could pass in, and so on until all had been in and passed back.

Not far from Jolo, out towards the foot of the mountains, is a coffee field. There are several others on the island besides that one. In these coffee fields a great many Morros work all the time gathering and cleaning coffee, etc. The method is like all others of theirs, very rude and poor. They dig out long troughs of wood and place them in running streams in such a way that the water will run in at one end and out at the other. Into these troughs the unhusked coffee is poured, and then it is tramped under the feet of the cleaners until the husks are all broken off and float away with the water. The coffee is then taken out and sacked and dried out for shipping. This is the only method I ever saw in use for coffee cleaning.

Tropical fruit is everywhere abundant. The bread fruit tree grows in Jolo to a great size. The fruit is about the size of a cocoanut, except it is of a flattened shape. It is covered by a thin soft hull easily cut open with an ordinary pocket knife. The first time that I ever saw the fruit I ate half of one. I thought it as good as anything I ever ate. I believe it will alone sustain life. Cocoanuts and bananas grow in profusion. Cocoanuts are cut and dried, then exported. Oil is manufactured of the dried cocoanuts, which is of excellent quality. We used it to oil our rifles all the time we were stationed in the Philippines. Chinese and natives caught quantities of fish, which were cut up and exposed to the sun several days to dry. The fish get almost black in this process of drying and smell badly before they are dry enough to be sacked and shipped. I saw a great deal of this business, but never learned where it was shipped to or what use was made of it.

Hemp is produced from a native plant growing wild in the forests, and looks something like the banana plant. It is baled and exported in great quantities. Natives bring in small bundles of it from the mountains. Red pepper grows abundantly in the woods on the high and dry lands. It grows on a small bush, which is loaded with the pods, which are very strong.

The natives in all the islands make a beverage of the dew which collects in the cocoanut buds. This dew and water stands in the buds and is collected early in the day. It is called tuba, and is liked by all the soldiers. I drank but little of it. I saw soldiers get drunk on it, and be crazy for a week.

## A Soldier in the Philippines

It is like all other beverages of the islands, but little is necessary to make a man drunk.

About twice every month we went out on a practice march for one day, only leaving about one company on guard. Every man would carry his dinner, and have almost a picnic, enjoying it much more than at other times and places, when we would be marched out in double time several miles and have a hard fight. We went out on these practice marches up the beach and returned across the mountains, stopping to rest frequently and gathering and eating cocoanuts. If any Morros were around we would give one a cent of Mexican money to climb the trees and get cocoanuts for us. The trees are hard to climb, but a Morro seems to climb them very easily. He will tie a piece of hemp just above his ankles and go right up a tree by jumps until the top is reached. Having secured the cocoanuts we would cut a hole in them and drink the icy water in them. This water is very nice and cold, and is particularly so to hot and tired soldiers.

When we would start out on what was a practice march most of the men would think we were going out to fight, and would not know differently until we returned, for it was generally known only to the officers where we were going or what the object of the march was. Sometimes we would have a long, hard march, and always through the woods and forests, for there were no roads. In the forest marches we frequently chased monkeys, of which the forests were full. We saw more monkeys in Jolo than in any other island we were on. Sometimes when three or four monkeys would discover us they would make a great noise, and, jumping from one tree to another, keep in one direction, and all the monkeys within my hearing would join in the procession, and keep up the noise and jumping. The trees would appear to be full of monkeys over us, all jumping in the same direction, and making a great noise. We amused ourselves and added to their trouble by throwing stones at them until they passed out of our line of march, which was frequently half an hour. The wild ones are hard to catch. Young ones, too young to climb well, were easily caught, and some were captured for pets.

Natives would catch them and sell them to the soldiers.

The Sultan of Jolo was fortified about ten miles across the mountains from Jolo. He lived in his fort with his army. My last practice march was made for the purpose of viewing the sultan's position, and to know something about his forces if we had to fight them. It was about ten o'clock on the morning of the 13th of May, 1900, when our commanding officer in great haste issued orders to get ready at once. We all thought we were going to fight that time. We were formed into a battalion as hastily as possible, under the commander's orders, who was present on his charger, and directing everything. We were soon moving out to no one seemed to know where, except our commander. No dinner was taken with us this time, only guns and as much ammunition as we could carry. We marched about five miles before halting for rest. It was very hot, and several soldiers fell out overcome by the heat. Some doubtless fell out to avoid a battle, as they thought. Two men just before me, whom I knew were great cowards, and who feared that we were going into a battle, decided that they could not face an enemy. I heard them talking about falling out ten or fifteen minutes. Their minds were made up to fall out and avoid fighting; one said that he would fall out if the other would stop to take care of him. This suited them exactly, and out they went, and were left behind. Our march was continued until we crossed the top of the mountain, and from the other side we could see the sultan's fort and trenches below us. It was then about three o'clock. We rested and looked at the sultan's fort, and looked over his position carefully. This was the object of the commander in marching us out there. He was expecting to have to fight the sultan, and decided that we should see his location and know as much as possible the conditions we would have to meet in fighting his forces. Returning we arrived in Jolo in the night.

## A Soldier in the Philippines

Our commander expected the sultan to attack our position, and wished to know just what to expect of us, and how quickly we could get into position to defend the fort. To ascertain this, and also to keep us in practice, a call to arms was given every month, when every man would get out and string around to the port holes in a very few minutes. Every soldier went as if he expected to have to fight. There were five companies of the Twenty-Third Regiment in Jolo while I was on duty there. Besides these one company was stationed in the Astoria block house, one company at Seassa and one at Buanga. These companies did not have as hard duty as the companies in Jolo, but every three months a company was sent to relieve one of these posts, and the relieved company would come into Jolo, where it could have the same duty and drill that the other companies had in Jolo. The companies at each of the three places just mentioned were relieved every three months.

Company E, of which I was a member, went to the Astoria block house about two months before we left Jolo and the Philippines. My company was doing guard duty at the block house when orders were received for recalling one battalion of the Twenty-Third Regiment, called the depot battalion, made up of sick men and those with less than six months' more service under their time of enlisting.

Those who had less than six months to serve were given the opportunity to stay or to return to the United States. I was not slow to accept the chance to return and was truly glad of the opportunity.

The transport *Warren* came to Jolo for the battalion on June 15th. The transport had come by the Island of Negros and Cebu, and took on board a battalion of soldiers who were going to return to the United States.

The "depot battalion" was made up of sick men and those who had short times. It was several days before we left Jolo. The men who were going as sick and disabled were examined by the physician. Those he believed could not endure the climate long and be able for duty, he recommended to be returned to the United States, and those who could endure the climate and proved to be healthy, stayed, unless they were of the class of short-time soldiers.

A man could not stand the climate of the Philippines many years unless he was very healthy and acquainted with tropical climates.

I do not believe the Philippines are a white man's country. I have heard doctors tell soldiers that if they stayed there, that five or six years would be as long as they could live.

Two friends and I had decided that when we served out our time that we would return to the United States by another route than that taken in going over, and thus make the trip around the world. We would go through the Mediterranean Sea to London and then to New York. But when the orders came that we could return on the government's time, and by a different route, we decided at once that we had seen enough of the world, and that the route taken by the transport would be long enough for us, and satisfy our thirst for travel.

The soldiers who had been taken on board from the islands of Negros and Cebu landed at Jolo, and went into camp, where they remained for eight days awaiting preparations of the soldiers at Jolo.

I was transferred from Company E to Company K on June 18th, and with those who were returning to the United States went into camp outside of the wall of Jolo in a cocoanut grove, where we stayed till the twenty-third day of June, when we boarded the transport *Warren* and sailed for Manila. Manila was reached on the morning of the twenty-sixth of June, where we stayed until the first day of July. A great many soldiers were added on at Manila, many wounded men and fifteen dead soldiers were put on to carry back to the United States, where the dead were sent to their relatives for burial.

While waiting a few days for all preparations to be made I obtained a pass and entered the city for the last time and viewed everything that was so familiar to me when on duty there.

It was during this short stop of only a few days that we heard of the trouble in China.

Three regiments of United States troops were immediately ordered to China: the Sixth, Ninth and Fourteenth Infantry then at Manila. The Ninth Infantry went on board the transport *Hancock*, which was lying alongside our transport, the *Warren*, and sailed just before us on its way to China.

A rumor was circulated that our transport was sailing to China, and that we were going there for service. A great many very foolishly believed the report.

July first the *Warren* sailed from Manila bound for San Francisco. The first day out from Manila, late in the evening when supper was eaten, I ate very heartily, and went on duty in the stern of the transport. The sea was rough, and gave the transport a rolling motion. Shortly after going on duty my head commenced swimming, and I was ill. A soldier told me that I was sea-sick. I had never been sea-sick and knew nothing about how a person felt. At last I vomited freely, and in less than an hour I was all right, except the swimming sensation of my head, which lasted a while longer. This little experience was all that I had in going over to the Philippines and returning to the United States.

The fourth day from Manila we arrived at Nagasaki, Japan. The following morning the transport was ready for inspection, the crew having worked most all night preparing for it. Every man on board and everything had to be inspected before we were allowed to enter the harbor. Nagasaki has a fine, deep harbor, where steamers and war vessels coal and take on supplies. Many large ships are in the harbor at all times.

The bay leading into the harbor is between hills which are almost entitled to the name of mountains. It is apparently a hilly and rough country to the traveler entering the bay to Nagasaki. On the left-hand side of the bay on entering is a large marble monument standing on the side of the hill. This is a monument in memory of Japan's first king. Of course I did not read the inscription, it being in Japanese; but the monument can be seen at a great distance. I learned about it from a resident of Nagasaki. While in Nagasaki I also learned that the Japanese are the hardest working, or rather the most industrious people, and receive the least compensation for their work of any race of people. Ten to fifteen cents per day is the regular price of labor. Several hundred are constantly employed in coaling vessels that enter the harbor. The coaling is done in a peculiar way. A line of men pass baskets filled with coal from one to another while the empty baskets are passed back to the place of filling by a line of children standing close enough to reach out one way and get a basket and pass it on to the next one standing on the other side; thus a continuous chain of baskets is kept going until the vessel is sufficiently coaled: the filled baskets going one way and the empty ones in the opposite direction. Men, women and children all work. Apparently no one is idle.

The lot of woman is extremely hard. A mother will fasten her child to her back and work all day with it there; sometimes it is asleep and sometimes it is yelling, but it is all the same to her. Children there do not receive the attention they get in America, but are handled roughly, and soon have to work, beginning work almost as soon as they can walk.

Hundreds of small boats, large enough to carry two or three people, are always ready to carry passengers to and from the ships and the landing for ten cents (Mexican). They are not allowed to charge more.

These small boats are provided with sides and a roof like a small house, into which passengers can go and close the door.

When you get ashore there are hundreds of little vehicles called jinrikishas, which look something like baby carriages with only one seat and an umbrella. The Japs will come trooping around jabbering to you to ride. You get in one and a Jap will get between a small pair of shafts and trot away with you, and go that way as long as you want him to for ten cents an hour. The traveler can go anywhere he desires in one of these vehicles. They do not use hacks and vehicles as Americans do. I never saw but one horse in Nagasaki. It was working to a dray, and was almost worked to death. The Jap's back seems to be his most convenient method, and almost the only one he has, of carrying anything.

Another soldier and I walked through the city looking at everything we could see. We soon discovered that almost every one was poking fun at us, all because we were walking instead of riding in jinrikishas. It seems that everybody there rides in them everywhere they go, and it appears funny to them to see anyone walking the streets. Peddlers are the exceptions, it seems, to this rule. A great many peddlers are seen walking the streets to vend their wares, and they have a great many articles that cannot be bought in America.

Every Japanese house has a rug or carpet on the floor— these are very nice articles. The funniest thing of all is the custom of stopping everybody at the door and have them take off their shoes before entering the house. They will not allow any one to enter their houses without pulling off his shoes. The reason of this, to my mind, is the fact that the rugs and carpets are made from grass and are very heavy, and catch dirt very easily.

## Chapter XII

THE JAPANESE ARE INDUSTRIOUS, good natured and friendly people. They treat every one kindly, and every one invited us to go into his house and chat awhile. Our greatest difficulty was to understand them. They appeared to be anxious to do anything they could for us, and considering everything as I could see it in our short stay, I believe I would like to live among them.

A great many Europeans are residents of Nagasaki. It is a fine town, a great deal of business is done there. The city is spread out along the bay back of the city, and all around the bay, except the entrance to it, are large hills, and on these a great many large guns are mounted. These natural barriers enable the Japanese to make the city a strongly fortified place. The government of Japan is good. Laws are rigid and strictly enforced. Theft is regarded as a very grave crime, and is punished with severe penalties.

Men with whom I talked in Nagasaki seemed to desire to leave the impression that Japan was well prepared for war, in fact better prepared than most any other country.

The transport *Warren* sailed from Nagasaki July ninth for San Francisco, taking the northern route of the Pacific Ocean. This route is claimed to be about two thousand miles longer than the southern route over which we sailed in going to Manila. The ocean currents and winds make a great deal of difference in which route a vessel is sailing in, and the northern and southern routes give the advantage to the vessels. Ships go the southern route from San Francisco to Manila and return the northern route.

After a few days out from Nagasaki we found colder water, which continued most of the way to San Francisco, only getting warmer a short distance from San Francisco. After getting out into this cold water the temperature of the atmosphere also fell, and every man who had an overcoat or even a heavy uniform put it on. Those who had only the thin uniforms called khaki worn in the Philippines, suffered from cold.

It was cold and disagreeable for all on board except the officers, who, as usual, fared well at all times and in all places.

There was a casual detachment of discharged soldiers numbering one hundred and thirty-eight on board, two hundred and forty-one officers and privates of the Twenty-third Regiment, sixty prisoners and twenty-one passengers, a total of four hundred and sixty men on board besides the crew. The transport *Warren* is a large vessel, and all on

## A Soldier in the Philippines

board had plenty of room.

Those men who were not thoughtful enough to start back to the United States with their heavy uniforms looked somewhat pitiful crowding around the engine rooms and boilers, and getting anywhere that offered some protection from the chilly air and sea breeze. I was fortunate in not being one of that number. I had plenty of warm clothing and fared well returning. I was on the lookout for myself, and provided myself with everything I desired, and had to call on no one for anything. My rule was to look out for myself all the time I was in the army, and usually I had everything I desired. If I wanted anything to use I always went where I could buy it, and never borrowed from the soldiers.

I always thought that was a good rule for a soldier; I noticed that those who did that fared much better than those who did not practice that rule.

I never liked to loan my gun and belt to a soldier when he has all those things of his own. But some soldiers would keep their guns polished and oiled, and set them away and borrow guns and belts from other soldiers to do guard duty with. These received the appellation of "orderly buckers" by their comrades, and were too lazy to walk post and perform a soldier's duty. Duty on the transport in returning to the United States was very hard on those soldiers who were well. Almost every soldier was on the sick report, and called by the soldiers the sick battalion. The few who were put on duty had it to perform every other night. I was one of the latter, and I considered it pretty tough too. Cooks on the transports were assigned for one year to cook for the soldiers. They were as filthy as hogs with everything they cooked. They cared nothing about how the rations were prepared nor how nasty they were, just so the cooking was over with as quickly as possible. They had no sympathy; anything seemed to the cooks good enough if it did not poison him. On our return we had plenty to eat if it had been cooked decently so that men could eat it. The reader may say that it should have been reported to the officer in command. This was done, and reported also to the officer of the day, and the next day after the reports were made we were given cabbage for dinner, and every man founds big worms in his plate of cabbage. While the officer of the day was passing by one soldier had the nerve to show him what was on his plate; immediately the officer of the day went to the cooks about it and that seemed to end it. One soldier found something in his plate that looked almost like a tarantula.

Some of the officers and a great many privates had a monkey apiece. Great care was taken of them by their owners. Two large monkeys belonged to some of the crew. These and the smaller ones had the whole vessel to run through and nothing escaped them—they were into everything. Finally the commanding officer gave orders for all the monkeys to be taken up, but the order was not carried out and he had the doctor chloroform the two large ones and throw them overboard. That made the crew very mad and sounded the death knell to all the monkeys on board.

That night the crew very quietly caught every monkey and threw them overboard—not one escaped. It was then the officers' turn to be mad and they did everything they could to learn who destroyed their monkeys. One old captain who had lost a monkey offered a reward of ten dollars to know who threw his monkey overboard, but he failed to find out who it was. I never heard such a fuss about as small a thing as a monkey before.

We arrived within one or two miles of the Golden Gate on July 3o. The transport stopped and the whistle was blown for the quarantine officers and a pilot. We could not see land, the fog was so heavy, until we got to the Golden Gate. The sight of land sent a thrill of gladness through every one on board, especially the soldiers who were beholding their own country, where they were soon to be discharged, and once more be free to go and come at their own pleasure. Just before night we went to the quarantine station on Angel Island and remained until morning, when everything was taken off the transport. On the first of August we went ashore at the Presidio wharf, landing in the evening.

We were not received as royally as we had departed, no

big reception was awaiting us, although I am quite sure the soldiers would have enjoyed one as much as when they were departing for the Philippines. I suppose it was thought that when we went away that we would never get back.

When we boarded the transport for the Philippines several thousand enthusiastic people witnessed our departure and a great display of patriotism was manifested. When that portion which returned when I did were landing only one woman and a little boy were present to show any feeling of rejoicing that we had not all perished in the Philippines from the awful climate and the Filipino bullets. This great patriotic display being over we went into camps at Presidio and remained there to rest and await further orders, which came in a few days, as soon as arrangements for transportation over the railroad could be made; and then Companies I and L went to Fort Douglas, Salt Lake City, Companies K and M were assigned to Fort D.A. Russell, Cheyenne, Wyoming. August sixth we left San Francisco and arrived at Fort D.A. Russell in the evening of August ninth. Companies K and M were under the command of Captain Delair, who is a good officer. Captain Devore had command of Company K, to which I then belonged and I remained with that company until discharged.

Captain Devore was a very good old religious kind of an officer, very strange and different from any other officer. The most that he believed in was to keep clean. He was very fond of seeing brooms, mops, picks and shovels in use. He liked to see work going on. He seemed to be too economical to eat as much as he needed of government rations. He would never allow any of the company's funds to be spent for any purpose, but was all the time adding to the fund.

The company was allowed twenty pounds of sugar every ten days. Of this Captain Devore would take off one pound for company funds. This is only one example, or illustration, of many ways of adding something to the funds of the company.

The company cook was preparing prunes one day for dinner when the old captain came around inspecting everything; the cook told him that he was cooking prunes. The cook was then asked how the men liked them, to which he was answered that the men would eat all that were being cooked and then not have more than half enough. The old captain said there were too many for the company—that six was enough for anyone. He further said, "I don't eat but two or three and that is as many as I want."

The company was always kicking about him. He was never pleased on inspection to find something cooking. He liked to find the stove cold and the cooking vessels all clean, then everything with him was O.K. He would give a man who had had a number of summary court martials an "excellent" discharge and some soldiers who were good duty soldiers and never had a court martial would get "only good." I have noticed that if he likes a soldier he will always get "excellent." He seemed never to be governed by a soldier's record. I had "very good," all I cared for, as I was so happy to get it.

I left the army November 11, 1900, en route to Dallas, Texas, where I remained a few days and went to Pleasant Point, where I spent several days with two of my brothers, John H. and Juney H. Freeman. Here I met many friends whom I had known before enlisting in the army and again I was free to join them in their sports as I had done before.

December twentieth, I started back to Georgia. I took the route via New Orleans, at which place I stopped about thirty hours and took another look at the old town. I wanted to look at it once more and compare it to the time when I was in camps there. I satisfied myself and proceeded on my homeward journey to the old red hills of Georgia, which I had left five years and two months before.

## THE END

## Further Reading

Honor in the Dust: *Theodore Roosevelt, War in the Philippines, and the Rise and Fall of America's Imperial Dream*, by Gregg Jones (New American Library, 2012)

Harper's Pictorial History of the War with Spain, Vol. II, by Nelson Appleton Miles, 1839-1925 (Public Domain, published 1899)
    downloadable in various formats at https://archive.org/details/harperspictorialoomilerich/page/n8/mode/1up